# Your One-stop Shop for
# Paper Crafting

From color and style to essential tools and stamping techniques, this all-in-one book will help boost your creativity when you need it most. After learning about color rules (including when to break them!), you'll be inspired with color combinations in bolds, pastels, neutrals, and jewel tones, and may even want to try your hand with some monochromatic color schemes. We've also put in a quick little quiz (p. 70) that will guide you to understand not only elements of various styles, but also which style appeals most to you. And once you have a handle on color and style, don't miss the comprehensive step-by-step lessons in stamping techniques starting on p. 143.

Before you get started, though, you'll want to take inventory of your paper crafting tool kit and be sure you have the essentials. Our must-haves are shown on p. 7 along with a listing of helpful uses for common tools and supplies. I'm sure your creativity will flow freely when you aren't hunting for a particular tool or supply to finish a project.

With designer tips and tricks plus a full index of projects by occasion (pgs. 190-191), this book is one that you'll find yourself using again and again.

Ultimately yours,

*Jennifer*

Because these projects are from past issues, some products may not be available. Luckily, the Internet provides a wonderful way to search for similar items so you can still create a beautiful project using these inspiring techniques. So, if you can't find a product, use your creativity to adapt the project and find a replacement.

p. 15

p. 109

p. 134

p. 77

p. 47

HAPPY BIRTHDAY

thank you

Mr. & Mrs.
AND THEY LIVED HAPPILY EVER AFTER

Love
is missing someone
whenever you're apart,
but somehow feeling warm inside
because you're close in heart.

OVER **1,000** PROJECTS, TIPS, TOOLS, & TECHNIQUES

# the ULTIMATE HANDBOOK for
# PAPER CRAFTERS

# the ULTIMATE HANDBOOK for PAPER CRAFTERS

## Editorial

Editor-in-Chief  Jennifer Schaerer
Managing Editor  Kerri Miller
Creative Editor  Susan R. Opel
Trends Editor  Cath Edvalson
Senior Editor  P. Kelly Smith
Online Editor  Holly Anderson
Editorial Assistant  Ahtanya Johnson

## Design

Art Director  Matt Anderson
Graphic Designer  Melinda Ward
Photography  bpd Studios

## Offices

Editorial
*Paper Crafts* magazine
14850 Pony Express Rd., Suite 200
Bluffdale, UT 84065-4801

Phone  801-816-8300

Fax  801-816-8302

E-mail  *editor@PaperCraftsMag.com*

Web site  *PaperCraftsMag.com*

Published by Leisure Arts, Inc., 5701 Ranch Drive, Little Rock, Arkansas 72223-9633. 501-868-8800. *www.leisurearts.com*

Library of Congress Control Number: 2012938936
ISBN-13: 978-1-4647-0052-1

## Leisure Arts Staff

Vice President of Editorial  Susan White Sullivan
Special Projects Director  Susan Frantz Wiles
Director of E-Commerce and Prepress Director  Mark Hawkins
Imaging Technician  Stephanie Johnson
Prepress Technician  Janie Marie Wright
Manager of E-Commerce  Robert Young
President and Chief Executive Officer  Rick Barton
Vice President of Sales  Mike Behar
Vice President of Finance  Laticia Mull Dittrich
National Sales Director  Martha Adams
Information Technology Director  Hermine Linz
Controller  Francis Caple
Vice President of Operations  Jim Dittrich
Retail Customer Service Manager  Stan Raynor
Vice President of Purchasing  Fred F. Pruss

## Creative Crafts Group, LLC

President and CEO:  Stephen J. Kent
VP/Group Publisher:  Tina Battock
Chief Financial Officer:  Mark F. Arnett
Controller:  Jordan Bohrer
IT Director:  Tom Judd
VP/Publishing Director:  Joel P. Toner
VP/Consumer Marketing:  Nicole McGuire
VP/Production & Technology:  Barbara Schmitz

## VISIT US ONLINE:

*PaperCraftsMag.com*
*PaperCraftsConnection.com*
*MoxieFabWorld.com*

 *facebook.com/papercraftsmagazine*

*twitter.com/papercraftsmag*

PUBLICATION—*Paper Crafts*™ (ISSN 1548-5706) (USPS 506250), is published 6 times per year in Jan/Feb, Mar/Apr, May/June, Jul/Aug, Sept/Oct and Nov/Dec, by Creative Crafts Group, LLC, 741 Corporate Circle, Suite A, Golden CO 80401. Periodicals postage paid at Salt Lake City, UT and additional mailing offices.

REPRINT PERMISSION—For information on obtaining reprints and excerpts, please contact Wright's Reprints at 877/652-5295. (Customers outside the U.S. and Canada should call 281/419-5725.)

TRADEMARKED NAMES mentioned in this book may not always be followed with a trademark symbol. The names are used only in an editorial fashion and to the benefit of the trademark owner, with no intention of infringement of the trademark.

PROJECTS—*Paper Crafts* magazine believes these projects are reliable when made, but none are guaranteed. Due to different climatic conditions and variations in materials, *Paper Crafts* disclaims any liability for untoward results in doing the projects represented. Use of the publication does not guarantee successful results. We provide this information WITHOUT WARRANTY OF ANY KIND, EXPRESSED, IMPLIED, OR STATUTORY; AND WE SPECIFICALLY DISCLAIM ANY IMPLIED WARRANTIES OF MERCHANTABILITY OR FITNESS FOR A PARTICULAR PURPOSE. Also, we urge parents to supervise young children carefully in their participation in any of these projects.

Posted under Canadian Publication Agreement Number 0551724

# Contents

p. 127

p. 61

PaperCraftsMag.com
PaperCraftsConnection.com

# Essential Tool Kit

Having everything at your fingertips will keep your creativity flowing freely – there's nothing more frustrating than hunting for a critical paper crafting tool while your project languishes, waiting to be completed.

❶ **Baby wipes** – great for cleaning stamps, hands, and work surface.

❷ **Cotton swabs** – apply paint, spread liquid adhesive, or even use them to create design elements on your projects.

❸ **Make-up sponge** – an economical solution for applying and blending ink.

❹ **Emery boards** – distress paper, reveal colored core of cardstock, or smooth edges of a decoupage element.

❺ **Paint brush** – brush away excess powder before heat embossing or whisk away stray glitter.

❻ **Stapler** – economical tool for adding a funky border or attaching bag toppers.

❼ **Permanent black marker** – trace around a stamped shape, add a handwritten sentiment, or darken a stamped image. Also excellent for labeling your tools with your name or initials.

❽ **White gel pen** – a must-have for adding faux stitching on colored cardstock.

❾ **Mechanical pencil** – sketch out a design before piercing, and the eraser is great for conditioning clear stamps before first use.

❿ **Mouse pad** – the perfect base for stamping and paper piercing.

⓫ **Medium Glue Dots** – use for adhering buttons and other dimensional embellishments.

⓬ **Repositionable glue stick** – great for temporarily adhering stamping masks or moving design elements before finishing your project.

⓭ **Fine point liquid adhesive** – adhere non-adhesive gems or the centers of pleated rosettes.

⓮ **General purpose glue stick** – perfect for paper-to-paper.

⓯ **Tape runner** – quick and easy for adhering pleated paper elements or ribbon.

⓰ **Small Zots** – smaller size is perfect for gems, small buttons, and tacking down the center of a ribbon bow.

⓱ **Two-way glue pen** – provides control for application on small pieces, and becomes repositionable when allowed to dry before adhering.

⓲ **Ballpoint glue pen** – trace intricate designs for heat embossing or use for adhering microscopic pieces.

⓳ **Scor-Tape** – double-sided adhesive that's perfect for pleating ribbon or creating your own washi tape with tissue paper.

⓴ **Foam tape** – add dimension to designs by adhering some pieces with it.

㉑ **Super tape** - high tack adhesive that sticks to just about anything.

㉒ **Craft Sheet** – collects overflow from spray mists, glitter application and embossing powder then wipes clean.

㉓ **Standard ¼" hole punch** – punch holes for threading ribbon or on gift tags.

㉔ **Crop-o-dile** – heavy-duty punch for chipboard and even metal. Also sets eyelets.

㉕ **Razor-point non-stick scissors** – a must for trimming anything with adhesive.

㉖ **General purpose scissors** – any small cuts or shape trimming.

㉗ **Easy action razor-point scissors** – prevent cramping when trimming intricate designs.

㉘ **Fine point tweezers** – pick up tiny gems or very small pieces of paper.

㉙ **Petal roller** – add a cupped shape to petals using the ball, and curl edges easily with the slotted end.

㉚ **Paper piercer** – add a pierced trail to a bee or butterfly or pre-pierce a stitched pattern before using needle and floss.

㉛ **Craft knife** – the best way to make straight cuts in chipboard.

㉜ **Swiveling craft knife** – perfect for intricate fussy-cutting on a curve.

㉝ **Mister** – blend inks on watercolor paper, mix pearlescent powders with water for an added sheen on paper, or moisten paper before stamping for an artistic look.

㉞ **Circle cutter** – cut circles in any increment between 1" and 8".

㉟ **Score Buddy** – create a clean fold in card bases or use for scoring folds to make boxes or bags.

# The New Color Rules
## ...Made to be Broken

## Rich tones for fall.
## Soft pastels for spring.
## No white before Memorial Day.

We've all heard the rules of color as they apply to fashion. And let's face it—our handmade cards are fashionable expressions of our personal styles. So how can we best understand how to use color stylishly and effectively in our cardmaking?

Our new color rules channel fashion's timeline, changing colors and textures with the seasons. But best of all—these are rules that are made to be followed and broken! Learn our guidelines, and then put your own spin on them for a colorful style that's all you!

## Bright & Bold

Think summer—flip flops, sarongs, and tanks in a rainbow of colors. Soak your cards in summertime boldness with fully-saturated tones that give your designs zing!

**Rule.** On their own, intense colors can overwhelm. Temper with neutrals like kraft, black, or white.

**Break it!** Ignore the rules and go totally intense with lush embellishments.

Rule

Break it

## Pretty Pastels

Get spring fever. Break out the soft shades, floaty fabrics, and girlish goodies that herald the return of warmer weather.

**Rule.** Pastels lend themselves well to the shabby chic style, so add inks and distressing for a vintage look.

**Break it!** Though the colors are graceful, a bold and linear design creates a completely different look that defies the rules.

Rule

Break it

## Jewel Tones

Fall for rich, deep autumnal hues. It's time for layering and cuddly sweaters and nature's palette.

**Rule.** Be aware of tonal differences – jewel colors are not as potent as brights. Make sure you pair them with embellishments that are somewhat de-saturated.

**Break it!** A smooth, streamlined look makes the colors pop when paired with a focal point outlined in white.

Rule

Break it

## Metallics

Come winter, our wardrobes take on a bit of sparkle and luster. Channel the holidays and the glistening, snow-covered landscape for projects that gleam.

**Rule.** Shiny papers such as glittered cardstock are ideal for elegant designs.

**Break it!** Who knew silver metallic could be cute? Ramp up the fun factor with red gingham ribbon and an adorable stamped sentiment.

Rule

Break it

## Monochromatic

A monochromatic scheme is a fashionable and flattering choice at any time of the year. Add a few neutral accessories, and you're well-dressed.

**Rule.** When designing with a single color, be sure to consider the mood the color conveys. For instance, red is a jubilant celebration of love.

**Break it!** Choose brown for a baby card with nary a pastel in sight by keeping design elements fun and cute.

Rule

Break it

## Neutrals

Seasonless and classic, neutrals are the staples of every closet.

**Rule.** A neutral color palette suits masculine cards well.

**Break it!** Feminine touches like fluttery butterflies and intricately punched borders play well with neutrals, too.

Rule

Break it

**DESIGNER TIP**

The stamps Beth used on this card came pre-inked so creating this dynamic design was super simple and speedy.

## ⑤ Feeling Perky

Designer: Beth Opel

❶ Make card from cardstock. Print sentiment on cardstock; trim into rectangle. ❷ Stamp circles. Punch circles from cardstock and adhere to piece with foam tape. *Note: Trim circles as needed.* ❸ Adhere piece to card with foam tape.

*Finished size: 3¼" x 4¼"*

## ⑤ Miss You Birdcage

Designer: Ryann Salamon

❶ Make card from cardstock; round bottom corners. ❷ Apply rub-on and affix stickers to spell "Miss you". ❸ Adhere green medallion with foam tape. Thread button with twine and adhere. ❹ Fold cardstock strip and adhere.

*Finished size: 3½" x 5½"*

**SUPPLIES:** *Cardstock:* (Palo Verde, Melon, Brick) Bazzill Basics Paper *Rubber stamps:* (dotted, star, sunburst circles from Round Trio set) 7gypsies *Fonts:* (Corbel) www. ascenderfonts.com; (CK Sassy) Creating Keepsakes *Tool:* (circle punch) Marvy Uchida

**SUPPLIES:** *Cardstock:* (Melon, Brick) Bazzill Basics Paper *Accents:* (green medallion) Making Memories; (melon button) Michaels *Rub-on:* (birdcage) E.A.D Designs *Stickers:* (Tiny Type alphabet) Making Memories *Fibers:* (black twine) May Arts *Tool:* (corner rounder punch) EK Success

## Damask Just Because

Designer: Lea Lawson

❶ Make card from cardstock. ❷ Die-cut cardstock and adhere to patterned paper rectangle. Adhere to card. ❸ Stamp just because on cardstock rectangle. Adhere cardstock strip. Border-punch patterned paper; adhere. ❹ Adhere scalloped border to stamped piece. Gather ribbon and adhere. Adhere rhinestone. ❺ Adhere piece to card with foam tape. ❻ Thread charms on twine and adhere.

*Finished size: 4¼" x 5½"*

## ⁵ₛₜₑₚₛ Treetop Hello

Designer: Kalyn Kepner

❶ Make card from cardstock. Adhere slightly smaller piece of cardstock. ❷ Stitch edges of cardstock rectangle. ❸ Die-cut treetops and trunks from cardstock; adhere. *Note: Adhere large tree with foam tape.* ❹ Stamp hello on journaling circle; adhere. Adhere buttons. ❺ Knot ribbon and adhere.

*Finished size: 4¼" x 5½"*

**SUPPLIES:** *Cardstock:* (Palo Verde, Melon, Brick) Bazzill Basics Paper *Patterned paper:* (Black Damask from Lush collection, Blossom Floating Flowers from Abbey Road collection) My Mind's Eye *Clear stamp:* (just because from Asian Fusion set) Papertrey Ink *Pigment ink:* (Onyx Black) Tsukineko *Accents:* (black scalloped border, rhinestone) Doodlebug Design; (orange, green, yellow heart charms) Maya Road *Fibers:* (red polka dot ribbon) Renaissance By Design; (natural twine) Darice *Die:* (large scalloped border) Papertrey Ink *Tool:* (border punch) Stampin' Up!

**SUPPLIES:** *Cardstock:* (Palo Verde, Melon, Beetle Black, Phoenix embossed) Bazzill Basics Paper *Clear stamp:* (hello from Mega Mixed Messages set) Papertrey Ink *Dye ink:* (black) Clearsnap *Accents:* (red buttons) Papertrey Ink *Sticker:* (journaling circle) October Afternoon *Fibers:* (green stitched ribbon) Offray; (red floss) DMC *Dies:* (small, large treetops; small, large trunks) QuicKutz

DESIGNER TIP

Bring attention to your sentiment by stamping a portion of it in a different color.

DESIGNER TIP

Customize this card by using your recipient's favorite colors.

### :5: It's a Girl

Designer: Latisha Yoast

❶ Make card from cardstock, round bottom corners, and adhere patterned paper strip. ❷ Tie on ribbon bow and adhere rhinestones. ❸ Stamp pennant banner on cardstock and patterned paper. Trim cardstock banner. Fussy-cut pennants from patterned paper and adhere to banner. ❹ Die-cut and emboss label from cardstock, stamp sentiment, and adhere to card with foam tape. ❺ Adhere banner with foam tape and attach clothespins.

*Finished size: 5½" x 4¼"*

### :5: Zipping By

Designer: Kim Kesti

❶ Make card from cardstock. ❷ Print sentiment on cardstock, trim into strip, and adhere zipper. Adhere piece to card. ❸ Adhere remaining zippers to cardstock strips and adhere to card.

*Finished size: 5¾" x 4"*

**SUPPLIES:** *Cardstock:* (white) Gina K Designs *Patterned paper:* (Luna, Earth from Hippy Girl collection) Kaisercraft *Clear stamps:* (sentiment from Sophie's Sentiments set, pennant banner from Bannerific set) Lawn Fawn *Dye ink:* (Tuxedo Black) Tsukineko *Specialty ink:* (Claret hybrid) Stewart Superior Corp. *Accents:* (natural mini clothespins) Hero Arts; (black rhinestones) Kaisercraft *Fibers:* (pink ribbon) Offray *Die:* (label) Spellbinders *Tool:* (corner rounder punch) Creative Memories

**SUPPLIES:** *Cardstock:* (Pink Fairy, Tangelo Blast, Lily White, Pepper embossed) Bazzill Basics Paper *Accents:* (assorted zippers) Wrights *Font:* (Stam Pete) www.dafont.com

DESIGNER TIPS

When designing cards with a grouping of similar elements, try adhering one element with foam tape to create depth and interest.

This design could be used as a teacher thank you or happy autumn card by simply switching the sentiment.

DESIGNER TIP

Adhere your white cardstock to chipboard before running it through the die cut machine. This makes your oval stronger and crisper looking.

##  Thank YOU

Designer: Angie Tieman

❶ Make card from cardstock; stamp scroll frame. ❷ Adhere patterned paper strip. Adhere ribbon. *Note: Pleat ribbon as you adhere.* ❸ Tie on ribbon bow. ❹ Die-cut oval from cardstock. Stamp thank you and adhere with foam tape. Attach paperclip.

*Finished size: 5½" x 4¼"*

## Bold Hi

Designer: Chan Vuong

❶ Make card from cardstock; adhere cardstock rectangle. ❷ Affix stickers to spell "Hi". ❸ Die-cut flower from cardstock; adhere with foam tape. Adhere button.

*Finished size: 3¼" x 5½"*

**SUPPLIES:** *Cardstock:* (Pumpkin Pie, Whisper White) Stampin' Up! *Patterned paper:* (Delectable from Delovely collection) Cosmo Cricket *Rubber stamps:* (scroll frame from Notably Ornate set, thank you from Engraved Greetings set) Stampin' Up! *Dye ink:* (Basic Black, Pixie Pink, Pumpkin Pie) Stampin' Up! *Accent:* (orange/pink floral paperclip) Cupcakes & Cartwheels *Fibers:* (orange ribbon) Stampin' Up!; (black ribbon) Offray *Die:* (oval) Ellison

**SUPPLIES:** *Cardstock:* (Lily White, Beetle Black, Bazzill Orange) Bazzill Basics Paper *Accent:* (pink button) *Stickers:* (Swing Into Spring alphabet) Bella Blvd *Die:* (flower) Provo Craft

## 5 Hooray!

Designer: Chan Vuong

1. Make card from cardstock; adhere patterned paper strips.
2. Stamp sentiment on cardstock rectangle, adhere twine, and adhere with foam tape.
3. Adhere pompom trim.

*Finished size: 5" x 3¾"*

## 5 To You

Designer: Vanessa Menhorn

1. Make card from cardstock; round corners and adhere ribbon.
2. Die-cut labels from cardstock; layer and adhere.
3. Trim stem and leaf from cardstock; adhere. Die-cut flower from felt; adhere.
4. Thread button with rickrack; adhere. Punch butterfly from cardstock; adhere.
5. Tie ribbon bow; adhere. Apply rub-on.

*Finished size: 4¼" x 5½"*

**SUPPLIES:** *Cardstock:* (Vintage Cream) Papertrey Ink *Patterned paper:* (orange gingham from Material Girl pad, Tossed Salad from Garden Variety collection) Cosmo Cricket; (Lily Child from Kioshi collection) BasicGrey *Clear stamp:* (sentiment from Fillable Frames #3 set) Papertrey Ink *Pigment ink:* (Onyx Black) Tsukineko *Fibers:* (yellow pompom trim) Michaels; (aqua/white string)

**SUPPLIES:** *Cardstock:* (Grape Slush, Lemon Drop, Bazzill Orange, Swimming Pool) Bazzill Basics Paper *Accent:* (teal button) Papertrey Ink *Rub-on:* (sentiment) Melissa Frances *Fibers:* (purple ribbon, yellow rickrack) Michaels *Dies:* (labels) Spellbinders; (flower) Papertrey Ink *Tools:* (butterfly punch) Martha Stewart Crafts; (corner rounder punch) *Other:* (yellow felt)

DESIGNER TIP

Curl up the bottom of your
sentiment for a more playful look

DESIGNER TIP

Look for inspiration in your mailbox!
This design was inspired by a pillow
in a home décor catalogue.

## 5 STEPS All Tied Up Birthday

Designer: Chan Vuong

❶ Make card from cardstock; round bottom corners. ❷ Wrap
twine around front flap. ❸ Stamp happy birthday on cardstock;
adhere with foam tape.

*Finished size: 3¾" x 5½"*

## 5 STEPS New Digs

Designer: Beth Opel

❶ Print sentiment on cardstock; fold into card. ❷ Punch patterned
paper circles, cut into fourths, and adhere to card with foam
tape. ❸ Cut slit in top of card. Thread ribbon and knot.
❹ Adhere rhinestones.

*Finished size: 6" x 4¼"*

**SUPPLIES:** *Cardstock:* (Yoyo Yellow) Stampin' Up!; (white) Papertrey Ink  *Clear
stamp:* (happy birthday from Just the Ticket set) Papertrey Ink  *Pigment ink:* (Onyx Black)
Tsukineko  *Fibers:* (orange, purple, aqua/white twine)  *Tool:* (corner rounder punch)
Marvy Uchida

**SUPPLIES:** *Cardstock:* (white) American Crafts  *Patterned paper:* (Cute Cuts from
Socialite collection) Bella Blvd; (Violet Dot from Double Dot collection) BoBunny Press;
(Tailored from Moda Bella collection) American Crafts; (Swimming Pool Filigree
from Sugar Coated collection) Doodlebug Design  *Accents:* (yellow rhinestones)
K&Company  *Fibers:* (purple ribbon) Offray  *Font:* (CBX Leen) Chatterbox  *Tool:* (circle
punch) EK Success

### Best Teacher

Designer: Latisha Yoast

① Make card from cardstock. ② Border-punch cardstock strip. Adhere cardstock strip and adhere panel to card with foam tape. ③ Die-cut and emboss circle from cardstock. Stamp lines, best, and teacher. Adhere with foam tape. ④ Stamp apple on cardstock, color with markers, trim, and adhere with foam tape. ⑤ Adhere pearls.

*Finished size: 4" x 5¼"*

### Hello Sunshine

Designer: Chan Vuong

① Make card from cardstock; adhere patterned paper and cardstock strips. ② Border-punch cardstock and adhere inside front flap. ③ Stamp hello sunshine on cardstock strip, curl edge, and adhere. ④ Affix sticker.

*Finished size: 4" x 5"*

**SUPPLIES:** *Cardstock:* (Parakeet, Bazzill Orange, Lily White) Bazzill Basics Paper *Clear stamps:* (best, teacher, lines, apple from School Basics set) i {heart} papers *Dye ink:* (Tuxedo Black) Tsukineko *Color medium:* (red, green markers) Copic *Accents:* (red pearls) Kaisercraft *Die:* (circle) Spellbinders *Tool:* (border punch) Fiskars

**SUPPLIES:** *Cardstock:* (Parakeet embossed) Bazzill Basics Paper; (Pure Poppy, white) Papertrey Ink *Patterned paper:* (Sunshine from Garden Variety collection) Cosmo Cricket *Clear stamp:* (hello sunshine from Fillable Frames #5 set) Papertrey Ink *Pigment ink:* (Onyx Black) Tsukineko *Sticker:* (carrot) Cosmo Cricket *Tool:* (border punch) EK Success

## :5: Blooming Thanks

Designer: Maile Belles

❶ Make card from cardstock. ❷ Stamp thanks, sunflower, and tulips on cardstock. Color with markers, and adhere. ❸ Tie ribbon bow around front flap and round corner. ❹ Adhere rhinestones.

*Finished size: 4¼" x 5½"*

## Thanks Teacher

Designer: Betsy Veldman

❶ Make card from cardstock; stitch border. ❷ Adhere patterned paper rectangle. Adhere patterned paper strips and stitch border. ❸ Adhere ribbon and tie on string bow. ❹ Die-cut notebook page from cardstock. Stamp ledger, alphabet border, and thanks teacher. Affix stickers and adhere to card. ❺ Stamp apple on cardstock; circle-punch. Punch flower from cardstock and attach with brad. ❻ Punch circles from cardstock and patterned paper. Trim patterned paper circle with decorative-edge scissors. ❼ Adhere circles together with foam tape and adhere to card.

*Finished size: 4¼" x 5½"*

**SUPPLIES:** *Cardstock:* (white) Papertrey Ink *Rubber stamps:* (sunflower, tulip, thanks from Thanks Flowers set) Hero Arts *Specialty ink:* (Noir hybrid) Stewart Superior Corp. *Color medium:* (red, orange, green markers) Copic *Accents:* (green rhinestones) Kaisercraft *Fibers:* (green ribbon) Michaels *Tool:* (corner rounder punch) EK Success

**SUPPLIES:** *Cardstock:* (Pure Poppy, white) Papertrey Ink *Patterned paper:* (Bee Mine from Love Bandit collection) BoBunny Press; (Measuring Up from Material Girl collection) Cosmo Cricket; (Mushroom Fancy from Twitterpated collection) Imaginisce; (Mixed Veggies from Vegetable Soup collection) Jillibean Soup *Clear stamps:* (alphabet border, apple, thanks teacher, ledger from School Time set) Papertrey Ink *Specialty ink:* (Pure Poppy, Ripe Avocado hybrid) Papertrey Ink *Accent:* (orange brad) Making Memories *Stickers:* (Delight alphabet) American Crafts *Fibers:* (green alphabet ribbon) Cosmo Cricket; (red/white string) Papertrey Ink *Die:* (notebook page) Papertrey Ink *Tools:* (circle punches) EK Success; (decorative-edge scissors) Provo Craft; (flower punch)

## Proud of You

Designer: Kalyn Kepner

❶ Make card from cardstock. Loop ribbon and adhere. ❷ Print sentiment on cardstock, trim, stitch edges, and adhere. ❸ Die-cut stars from cardstock, patterned paper, and transparency sheet. *Note: Emboss Beetle Black cardstock and adhere transparency sheet to cardstock before die-cutting.* ❹ Adhere stars to card, using foam tape as desired. ❺ Thread button with floss; adhere. Adhere remaining buttons.

*Finished size: 4¼" square*

## Special Delivery

Designer: Betsy Veldman

*Ink all paper edges.*
❶ Make card from cardstock. ❷ Die-cut postage stamp from cardstock, trim card from patterned paper, and adhere. Zigzag-stitch side and affix stickers. ❸ Die-cut ticket and star from cardstock. Stamp Postage Cancellation, star ticket, and special delivery on die cut ticket. Adhere star and ticket. ❹ Ink chipboard wings; adhere. Thread button with sting; adhere. ❺ Double-mat piece with cardstock and patterned paper. Tie with string bow and adhere to card.

*Finished size: 4¼" x 5"*

**SUPPLIES:** *Cardstock:* (Bazzill Red, Sea Water, Lily White, Beetle Black) Bazzill Basics Paper *Patterned paper:* (Vintage Plaid from June Bug collection) BasicGrey *Transparency sheet:* (black houndstooth) Hambly Screen Prints *Accents:* (red, white, blue buttons) Papertrey Ink *Fibers:* (red stitched ribbon) Papertrey Ink; (red floss) DMC *Fonts:* (Chopin Script, Bodoni Hand) www.dafont.com *Template:* (embossing Swiss Dots) Provo Craft *Die:* (star) QuicKutz

**SUPPLIES:** *Cardstock:* (Spring Rain, Pure Poppy, white) Papertrey Ink *Patterned paper:* (Cards from About a Girl collection) Fancy Pants Designs; (Vintage Jane from Homespun Chic collection) GCD Studios *Clear stamps:* (special delivery from Night, Night Moon set; star ticket from Just the Ticket set) Papertrey Ink; (Postage Cancellation) Studio Calico *Pigment ink:* (Spring Rain) Papertrey Ink *Chalk ink:* (Creamy Brown) Clearsnap *Specialty ink:* (Pure Poppy, True Black hybrid) Papertrey Ink *Accents:* (red button) Papertrey Ink; (chipboard wings) Bisous *Stickers:* (baby boy, star border) Little Yellow Bicycle *Fibers:* (red/white string) Papertrey Ink *Dies:* (ticket) Papertrey Ink; (postage stamp, star) Provo Craft

## Love You

Designer: Alicia Thelin

❶ Make card from cardstock; adhere cardstock strip. ❷ Border-punch cardstock; adhere. Zigzag-stitch seam. ❸ Die-cut heart from patterned paper; adhere. Apply rub-on. ❹ Adhere stick pins between buttons and pearls. Tie with ribbon and adhere. ❺ Slot-punch card, trim cardstock strip, thread through slot, and staple.

*Finished size: 4¼" x 5½"*

## Shabby Miss You

Designer: Julia Stainton

*Ink all edges.*
❶ Make card from cardstock; adhere die cut. *Note: Trim excess die cut.* ❷ Adhere patterned paper strip. ❸ Fold and ink cardstock strip; staple to card. Apply rub-on. ❹ Affix stickers. ❺ Thread buttons with string and adhere. *Note: Sand buttons before adhering.*

*Finished size: 5½" x 4¼"*

**SUPPLIES:** *Cardstock:* (Real Red, Bashful Blue) Stampin' Up!; (white embossed) DCWV Inc. *Patterned paper:* (Life Measured from Documented collection) Teresa Collins Designs *Accents:* (white pearls) Stampin' Up!; (red, blue buttons) Oriental Trading Co.; (silver stick pins, staples) *Rub-on:* (love you) Stampin' Up! *Fibers:* (red gingham ribbon) Stampin' Up! *Die:* (heart) Provo Craft *Tools:* (border, slot punches) Stampin' Up!

**SUPPLIES:** *Cardstock:* (Raven, Sea Water) Bazzill Basics Paper *Patterned paper:* (Fly a Kite from Hello Sunshine collection) Lily Bee Design *Dye ink:* (brown) *Accents:* (red, blue buttons) BasicGrey; (graph die cut) Lily Bee Design; (silver mini staples) Tim Holtz *Rub-on:* (miss you circle) Maya Road *Stickers:* (newsprint flowers) Lily Bee Design *Fibers:* (red/white string)

## ⟨5⟩ For Your Friendship

Designer: Kelley Eubanks

❶ Make card from cardstock; round bottom corners. ❷ Stamp flowers; emboss. ❸ Stamp sentiment and adhere rhinestones.

*Finished size: 5½" x 4¼"*

## ⟨5⟩ Happy Birthday to You

Designer: Julia Stainton

❶ Make card from cardstock; adhere cardstock rectangles. ❷ Apply sentiment rub-on to cardstock rectangle, mat with cardstock, and adhere. ❸ Apply flower rub-ons. Adhere rhinestones and flower.

*Finished size: 4¼" x 5½"*

**SUPPLIES:** *Cardstock:* (white) Papertrey Ink *Rubber stamps:* (flowers, sentiment from Upsy Daisy set) Stampin' Up! *Pigment ink:* (Red Magic) Tsukineko *Watermark ink:* Tsukineko *Embossing powder:* (Lavender) American Crafts *Accents:* (green rhinestones) Kaisercraft *Tool:* (corner rounder punch) Stampin' Up!

**SUPPLIES:** *Cardstock:* (Spring Breeze, Lavender Twilight, Kisses, Lily White) Bazzill Basics Paper *Accents:* (red sequin flower) Prima; (green, clear rhinestones) BasicGrey *Rub-ons:* (flowers, sentiment) BasicGrey

## :5: Here to There

Designer: Teri Anderson

❶ Make card from cardstock. ❷ Stamp clouds on cardstock, trim, and adhere. ❸ Stamp cityscape, farm, and suburbia on cardstock, trim, and adhere. ❹ Stamp sentiment on card and adhere rhinestones.

*Finished size: 5½" x 4¼"*

## :5: Welcome Baby

Designer: Lisa Johnson

❶ Make card from cardstock. ❷ Stamp moon/star border on cardstock rectangle; round top corners and ink edges. ❸ Adhere ribbon and string. Die-cut scalloped border from cardstock and adhere to piece. Adhere to card with foam tape. ❹ Stamp stars, welcome, and baby on cardstock. Punch into circle and adhere with foam tape. ❺ Tie ribbon bow and adhere. Adhere knotted string.

*Finished size: 4¼" x 5½"*

**SUPPLIES:** *Cardstock:* (Spring Breeze, Lavender Twilight, Kisses, Lily White) Bazzill Basics Paper *Rubber stamp:* (Clouds) A Muse Artstamps *Clear stamps:* (sentiment, cityscape, farm, suburbia from Neighborhood set) My Stamp Box *Dye ink:* (Real Red) Stampin' Up! *Pigment ink:* (Spring Moss) *Specialty ink:* (Lavender Moon hybrid) Papertrey Ink *Accents:* (red rhinestones) Kaisercraft

**SUPPLIES:** All supplies from Papertrey Ink unless otherwise noted. *Cardstock:* (Spring Breeze) Bazzill Basics Paper; (Almost Amethyst) Stampin' Up!; (Pure Poppy, white) *Clear stamps:* (welcome, baby, star, moon/star border from Night, Night Moon set) *Dye ink:* (Almost Amethyst) Stampin' Up! *Pigment ink:* (Fresh Snow) *Watermark ink:* Tsukineko *Specialty ink:* (Pure Poppy hybrid) *Fibers:* (white ribbon, red/white string) *Die:* (small scalloped border) *Tools:* (corner rounder, circle punches) Marvy Uchida

DESIGNER TIP

Don't be afraid to use accents as unexpected pops of color.

## Love Blooms

Designer: Ashley C. Newell

❶ Make card from cardstock; ink edges. ❷ Stamp borders on cardstock rectangle; emboss. Zigzag-stitch to card. ❸ Trim leaves from patterned paper; adhere. Adhere flower. ❹ Stamp love blooms on cardstock, trim, and adhere.

*Finished size: 4¼" x 8¼"*

## Spread Sunshine

Designer: Julia Stainton

❶ Make card from cardstock. Adhere felt flourish and zigzag-stitch. ❷ Stamp spread sunshine on cardstock strip; adhere with foam tape. ❸ Adhere flower.

*Finished size: 5½" x 4¼"*

**SUPPLIES:** *Cardstock:* (white, kraft) Papertrey Ink *Patterned paper:* (green grid) *Clear stamps:* (lace borders from Borderline Vintage Lace set) Technique Tuesday; (love blooms from Favor It Weddings set) Papertrey Ink *Dye ink:* (Antique Linen) Ranger Industries *Pigment ink:* (Spanish Moss) Tsukineko *Watermark ink:* Tsukineko *Embossing powder:* (white) Stampendous! *Accent:* (yellow flower with rhinestones) Prima

**SUPPLIES:** *Cardstock:* (Petty Cash shimmer, Champagne) Bazzill Basics Paper *Clear stamp:* (spread sunshine from Anytime Messages set) Hero Arts *Dye ink:* (Jet Black) Ranger Industries *Accents:* (yellow flower) Maya Road; (white felt flourish) Prima

## Together

Designer: Angie Tieman

❶ Make card from cardstock; emboss. ❷ Stamp chairs and together definition on cardstock rectangle, round corners, and adhere with foam tape. ❸ Die-cut scalloped border from wool ribbon; adhere. Thread button with string and adhere.

*Finished size: 4¼" square*

## With Sympathy

Designer: Kelley Eubanks

❶ Make card from cardstock. ❷ Apply rub-on to cardstock square. Stamp sentiment; emboss. ❸ Round corner of piece, ink edges, and adhere with foam tape. ❹ Adhere pearls and tie on ribbon bow.

*Finished size: 4½" square*

**SUPPLIES:** All supplies from Stampin' Up! unless otherwise noted. *Cardstock:* (Crumb Cake, Whisper White) *Rubber stamps:* (together definition from Define Your Life set, chairs from Have a Seat set) *Dye ink:* (So Saffron, Crumb Cake) *Accent:* (green button) *Fibers:* (white string, yellow wool ribbon) no source *Template:* (embossing polka dots) Ellison *Die:* (large scalloped border) Papertrey Ink *Tool:* (corner rounder punch)

**SUPPLIES:** *Cardstock:* (Petty Cash shimmer, Candlelight) Bazzill Basics Paper *Clear stamp:* (sentiment from Mega Mixed Messages set) Papertrey Ink *Pigment ink:* (Wheat) Tsukineko *Embossing powder:* (clear) Stewart Superior Corp. *Accents:* (taupe pearls) Prima *Rub-on:* (flourished label) Hambly Screen Prints *Fibers:* (white ribbon) May Arts *Tool:* (corner rounder punch) Stampin' Up!

**DESIGNER TIP**

Draw the vine with a glue pen and then adhere the string for a perfectly curly accent.

## 5 Always & Forever

Designer: Latisha Yoast

1 Make card from cardstock. Adhere patterned paper. 2 Border-punch patterned paper strip and adhere. 3 Adhere flower and rhinestones. 4 Affix stickers to spell "Always & Forever".

*Finished size: 6" x 3¼"*

## 5 Birthday Wishes

Designer: Kim Hughes

1 Make card from cardstock. Mat cardstock square with cardstock and adhere. 2 Stamp birthday wishes on cardstock rectangle. Round top corners and trim with decorative-edge scissors. 3 Adhere cardstock strip to piece and adhere to card. 4 Trim leaves from cardstock; fold slightly and adhere. Punch flowers from patterned paper; adhere. 5 Thread button with floss and adhere. Adhere string.

*Finished size: 4¼" square*

**SUPPLIES:** *Cardstock:* (Petty Cash shimmer) Bazzill Basics Paper *Patterned paper:* (Cornflowers from Fresh Print Clothesline collection) Little Yellow Bicycle; (Beautiful So Cute from Quite Contrary collection) My Mind's Eye *Accents:* (layered flower with button) BasicGrey; (green rhinestones) Kaisercraft *Stickers:* (Tiny Alpha alphabet) Making Memories *Tool:* (border punch) Fiskars

**SUPPLIES:** *Cardstock:* (Petty Cash shimmer, Steel Blue, Baby Pink Medium, Lily White) Bazzill Basics Paper *Patterned paper:* (Cupcake Serenade from Sugar Coated collection) Doodlebug Design *Clear stamps:* (birthday wishes from Big Wish set) Verve Stamps *Dye ink:* (Indian Corn Blue) Close To My Heart *Accent:* (pink button) Papertrey Ink *Fibers:* (pink floss) DMC; (green/white string) *Dies:* (small, medium flowers) The Cat's Pajamas *Tools:* (corner rounder punch) Fiskars; (decorative-edge scissors)

DESIGNER TIP

Use a piece of scalloped-
edge cardstock as a template
for cutting decorative edges
on your patterned paper.

DESIGNER TIPS

Customize flowers by sponging them
with ink or spritzing them with dye
ink shimmer sprays.

Flourishes are great for tying together
various layers on a paper project.

## Loveliest of Birthdays

Designer: Beth Opel

❶ Make card from cardstock; adhere patterned paper. ❷ Cut scallops from patterned paper strip; adhere. ❸ Adhere trim and accent scallops with glitter glue. ❹ Create sentiment using software and fonts, print on cardstock, and adhere. ❺ Adhere chipboard frame and flowers. Insert stick pin.

*Finished size: 5½" x 4"*

## Green Get Well

Designer: Julia Stainton

❶ Make card from cardstock. ❷ Adhere cardstock and patterned paper rectangles. ❸ Stamp sentiment and adhere pearl flourish. ❹ Ink edges of flower, insert brad, and adhere.

*Finished size: 5½" x 4¼"*

**SUPPLIES:** *Cardstock:* (Lily White) Bazzill Basics Paper *Patterned paper:* (With Love from Letterbox collection) American Crafts; (Passion Fruit Dot from Double Dot collection) BoBunny Press *Accents:* (white pearl stick pin) Maya Road; (pink flowers) Prima; (white chipboard frame) American Crafts; (iridescent glitter glue) Ranger Industries *Fibers:* (white trim) Jo-Ann Stores *Fonts:* (Arabella) www.dafont.com; (Algerian) www.fonts.com *Software:* (word processing)

**SUPPLIES:** *Cardstock:* (Lily White, Steel Blue) Bazzill Basics Paper *Patterned paper:* (Whimsy from Lovely collection) Lily Bee Design *Clear stamp:* (sentiment from Leaf Prints set) Hero Arts *Dye ink:* (Jet Black, Worn Lipstick) Ranger Industries *Accents:* (white flower) Prima; (blue pearl flourish) Zva Creative; (green floral brad) BasicGrey

DESIGNER TIP

Mix fonts like an expert—combine serif and sans-serif, upper and lower case, bold and regular fonts for a professional look every time.

## You Can Do It

Designer: Julia Stainton

❶ Make card from cardstock. ❷ Mat patterned paper with cardstock and adhere. ❸ Accent butterfly with pen and adhere with foam tape. ❹ Apply rub-on to cardstock, punch into circle, and trim edge. Staple to card.

*Finished size: 4½" square*

## Pretty Girl

Designer: Beth Opel

❶ Make card from cardstock; trim 1" from front flap. ❷ Adhere pink scalloped border behind front flap. ❸ Create sentiment with fonts and software, print on cardstock, round left corners, and adhere. ❹ Border-punch cardstock; adhere. Adhere pearls. ❺ Adhere ribbon. Trim scalloped circles from cardstock, tie on twine bows, and adhere with foam tape. ❻ Trim doilies from border sticker; affix. Adhere rhinestones.

*Finished size: 4½" x 5½"*

**SUPPLIES:** *Cardstock:* (Champagne, Razzleberry Light, Lily White) Bazzill Basics Paper *Patterned paper:* (Rose McGrain from Craft Fair collection) American Crafts *Color medium:* (white pen) Ranger Industries *Accents:* (butterfly) K&Company; (silver mini staples) Tim Holtz *Rub-on:* (sentiment) Melissa Frances *Tool:* (circle punch) EK Success

**SUPPLIES:** *Cardstock:* (Champagne, Scallop Bazzill White) Bazzill Basics Paper; (Dusty Pink) SEI *Accents:* (white pearls) Kaisercraft; (pink rhinestones) Martha Stewart Crafts; (pink scalloped border) Doodlebug Design *Sticker:* (pink doily border) Little Yellow Bicycle *Fibers:* (tan polka dot ribbon, natural twine) SEI *Fonts:* (Metro) www.searchfreefonts.com; (Baskerville Old Style) www.fonts.com *Software:* (word processing) *Tools:* (corner rounder punch) EK Success; (border punch) Fiskars

DESIGNER TIP
Create custom backgrounds by combining your favorite stamped images.

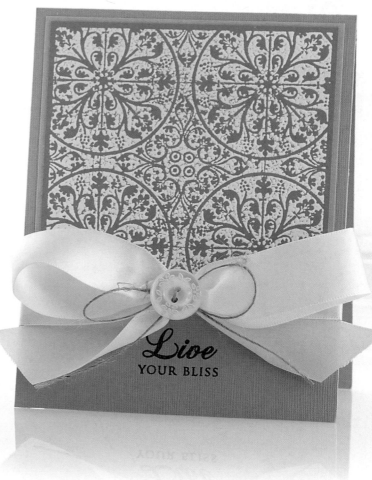

## Butterfly Congrats

Designer: Sarah Martina Parker

*Ink all edges.*

❶ Make card from cardstock; stamp congrats. ❷ Stamp flowers and circles on cardstock; zigzag-stitch to card. ❸ Tie on ribbon bow. ❹ Die-cut label from patterned paper; adhere with foam tape. Adhere butterfly, rhinestones, and buttons.

*Finished size: 4¼" x 5½"*

## Live Your Bliss

Designer: Windy Robinson

❶ Make card from cardstock. ❷ Stamp Ancient Motif on cardstock; emboss. Mat with cardstock and adhere. ❸ Stamp sentiment. ❹ Tie ribbon bow around front flap and tie button on with twine.

*Finished size: 4¼" x 5½"*

**SUPPLIES:** *Cardstock:* (Mauve Ice) Bazzill Basics Paper; (white) Papertrey Ink *Patterned paper:* (Very Berry from Pink Plum collection) Crate Paper *Clear stamps:* (congrats from Essential Messages set) Hero Arts; (flower from Giga Guide Lines set, circle from Round & Round set) Papertrey Ink *Pigment ink:* (Fresh Snow, Hibiscus Burst) Papertrey Ink *Pigment ink:* (Wheat) Tsukineko *Accents:* (brown buttons) Papertrey Ink; (pink rhinestones) My Mind's Eye; (white butterfly) *Fibers:* (pink ribbon) MemrieMare *Die:* (label) Papertrey Ink

**SUPPLIES:** *Cardstock:* (Champagne, Mauve Ice, Razzleberry Light) Bazzill Basics Paper *Rubber stamp:* (Ancient Motif) Hero Arts *Clear stamps:* (sentiment from Mega Mixed Messages set) Papertrey Ink *Pigment ink:* (Vintage Sepia) Tsukineko; (white) Stampin' Up! *Embossing powder:* (white) Jo-Ann Stores *Accent:* (white button) Tim Holtz *Fibers:* (natural twine) May Arts; (white ribbon) Michaels

## You Did It!

Designer: Lisa Johnson

❶ Make card from cardstock. ❷ Die-cut eyelet borders from cardstock; adhere. ❸ Die-cut notebook page from cardstock, stamp lines and sentiment, and adhere with foam tape. ❹ Stamp arrow on cardstock; trim and adhere. ❺ Punch stars from cardstock; adhere with foam tape. ❻ Adhere sequins and rhinestones.

*Finished size: 4¼" x 5½"*

## Floral Get Well Wishes

Designer: Sarah Martina Parker

❶ Make card from cardstock; ink edges. ❷ Zigzag-stitch patterned paper to card. ❸ Stamp sentiment and affix sticker. ❹ Adhere leaves and flowers. Tie ribbon bow and adhere.

*Finished size: 4¼" x 5½"*

**SUPPLIES:** *Cardstock:* (Caribbean Breeze, Petty Cash shimmer, Mango, Candlelight) Bazzill Basics Paper *Clear stamps:* (arrow from Get to the Point set, sentiment from Signature Greetings set, lines from School Time set) Papertrey Ink *Pigment ink:* (Fresh Snow) Papertrey Ink *Watermark ink:* Tsukineko *Specialty ink:* (True Black hybrid) Papertrey Ink *Accents:* (clear rhinestones) Zva Creative; (teal sequins) Michaels *Dies:* (notebook page, eyelet border) Papertrey Ink *Tool:* (star punch) EK Success

**SUPPLIES:** *Cardstock:* (Lily White) Bazzill Basics Paper *Patterned paper:* (Fringe from Restoration collection) Crate Paper *Clear stamp:* (sentiment from Fancy Phrases set) Waltzingmouse Stamps *Dye ink:* (Tea Dye) Ranger Industries *Pigment ink:* (Turquoise Gem) Tsukineko *Accents:* (yellow, teal, taupe flowers) Prima; (green leaves) Michaels *Sticker:* (frame) Crate Paper *Fibers:* (teal ribbon) MemrieMare

Think outside the box with your sticker stash.
This alligator sticker is part of a baby collection,
but becomes a fun child's birthday card when
paired with a punny sentiment.

## Rock-a-Bye Baby
Designer: Kalyn Kepner

❶ Make card from cardstock. Trim cardstock square with
decorative-edge scissors, stitch edges, and adhere. ❷ Trim moon
from cardstock, stitch edges, and mat with cardstock. Adhere
with foam tape. ❸ Die-cut stars from cardstock; adhere. Thread
buttons with floss; adhere. ❹ Write sentiment with pen.

*Finished size: 4¾" square*

## Snappy Birthday
Designer: Betsy Veldman

❶ Make card from cardstock. ❷ Die-cut rickrack from cardstock;
adhere to patterned paper rectangle. Mat piece with patterned
paper. ❸ Adhere patterned paper strip, stitch edges, and adhere
to card. ❹ Affix birthday sticker and spell "Snappy" with alphabet
stickers. ❺ Die-cut flower from felt; adhere. ❻ Affix alligator
sticker to patterned paper, trim with decorative-edge scissors, and
adhere. Thread buttons with string and adhere.

*Finished size: 3¾" x 5¼"*

**SUPPLIES:** *Cardstock:* (Caribbean Breeze, Petty Cash shimmer, Mango, Candlelight)
Bazzill Basics Paper *Color medium:* (white ink) *Accents:* (yellow, orange, green
buttons) Papertrey Ink *Fibers:* (yellow, orange, green floss) DMC *Dies:* (stars) QuicKutz
*Tool:* (decorative-edge scissors) Fiskars

**SUPPLIES:** *Cardstock:* (Petty Cash shimmer) Bazzill Basics Paper *Patterned paper:*
(graph from Rusted Sun pad) Fancy Pants Designs; (Fireflies from Fly a Kite collection)
October Afternoon; (Josephine from Madame Royale collection) We R Memory
Keepers; (Rob Roy from Lime Rickey collection) BasicGrey *Accents:* (orange buttons)
Papertrey Ink *Stickers:* (birthday) SRM Press; (crocodile) Little Yellow Bicycle; (Whoo-
ligans alphabet) BoBunny Press *Fibers:* (blue/white string) Papertrey Ink *Dies:* (rickrack,
flower) Papertrey Ink *Tool:* (decorative-edge scissors) Provo Craft *Other:* (yellow felt)
Papertrey Ink

## Sending You

Designer: Betsy Veldman

① Make card from cardstock; adhere patterned paper. ② Adhere patterned paper strips and lace. Stitch borders. ③ Stamp sending you, birthday wishes, flowers, and dots. ④ Die-cut postage stamp from cardstock. Stamp Postage Cancellation. Trim square from piece, ink edges, and adhere. *Note: Adhere square with foam tape.* ⑤ Tie button to card with twine.

*Finished size: 6" x 3½"*

## Love Always

Designer: Laura O'Donnell

① Make card from cardstock. Stamp branch and love always. ② Open two birds in software; resize one and flip. Print on cardstock. ③ Trim birds and adhere with foam tape.

*Finished size: 4" square*

**SUPPLIES:** *Cardstock:* (Vintage Cream) Papertrey Ink *Patterned paper:* (Fairy Rings, pin stripe from Pixie-Licious pad) Cosmo Cricket; (Happy Birthday Grown Up from Quite Contrary collection) My Mind's Eye *Clear stamps:* (sending you from Big & Bold Wishes set; birthday wishes from Vintage Picnic Sentiments set; flowers, dots from Beautiful Blooms II set) Papertrey Ink; (Postage Cancellation) Studio Calico *Dye ink:* (Orchid Opulence) Stampin' Up! *Pigment ink:* (Raspberry Fizz, Sweet Blush) Papertrey Ink *Accent:* (purple button) Papertrey Ink *Fibers:* (cream twine) Papertrey Ink; (pink lace) Fancy Pants Designs *Die:* (postage stamp) Provo Craft

**SUPPLIES:** *Cardstock:* (Lupine, Lily White) Bazzill Basics Paper *Clear stamps:* (love always from All Occasion Messages set, branch from Kiss from the Sun set) Hero Arts *Dye ink:* (Tuxedo Black) Tsukineko *Digital element:* (pink bird from Cute & Wild Stickers kit) www.twopeasinabucket.com *Software:* (photo editing)

## 5 STEPS So Glad

Designer: Erin Lincoln

❶ Make card from cardstock; adhere patterned paper. ❷ Stamp sentiment, friends, and scrolls on patterned paper. ❸ Die-cut mirror, dress forms, and dresses from cardstock. Adhere stamped piece behind mirror and adhere to card. ❹ Emboss and deboss dresses. Adhere dress forms and dresses. ❺ Adhere flowers and rhinestones.

*Finished size: 4¼" x 6"*

## 5 STEPS Heartfelt Baby

Designer: Kim Hughes

❶ Make card from cardstock; round opposite corners. ❷ Adhere patterned paper rectangles. *Note: Round opposite corners before adhering.* ❸ Trim heart from cardstock; adhere. ❹ Tie string bow around front flap. Adhere flower and insert brad. ❺ Affix stickers to spell "Baby".

*Finished size: 5½" x 4¼"*

**SUPPLIES:** *Cardstock:* (Lupine, Baby Pink Light, Intense Pink) Bazzill Basics Paper *Patterned paper:* (Golden Gleam from Dear Lizzy collection) American Crafts; (Pink Floral from Lush collection) My Mind's Eye *Clear stamps:* (sentiment, friends from Friends 'Til the End set; scroll from Vintage Labels set) Papertrey Ink *Pigment ink:* (Plum Pudding) Papertrey Ink *Specialty ink:* (True Black hybrid) Papertrey Ink *Accents:* (pink, purple flowers with rhinestones) K&Company; (clear rhinestones) *Templates:* (embossing polka dots) Provo Craft; (debossing diamonds) Papertrey Ink *Dies:* (dress form, dress, mirror) QuicKutz

**SUPPLIES:** *Cardstock:* (Blissful embossed) Bazzill Basics Paper; (purple) Core'dinations *Patterned paper:* (Pansy Trim from Fresh Print Clothesline collection) Little Yellow Bicycle; (Hearts Bloom from Cupid collection) Pink Paislee *Accents:* (pink brad) BasicGrey; (purple flower) Prima *Stickers:* (Giggles alphabet) American Crafts *Fibers:* (pink/white string) *Tool:* (corner rounder punch) Fiskars

BONUS IDEA

Instead of rhinestones, use cardstock or patterned paper for the center of the flowers.

## Enjoy the Ride

Designer: Beth Opel

❶ Make card from cardstock. ❷ Stamp 1957 Bel Air repeatedly on cardstock. Punch right edge and adhere. ❸ Trim and adhere cardstock strips. ❹ Print sentiment on cardstock. Punch into circle and mat with punched cardstock circle. Adhere with foam tape.

*Finished size: 6" x 3"*

## Birthday Wishes

Designer: Lea Lawson

❶ Make card from cardstock. ❷ Die-cut scallop from patterned paper panel. ❸ Stamp birthday wishes and flowers on cardstock. Adhere rhinestones. ❹ Mat with patterned paper panel and tie on ribbon. ❺ Adhere panel with foam tape.

*Finished size: 4¼" x 5½"*

**SUPPLIES:** *Cardstock:* (Jubilee, Shamrock, Desert Marigold, Breaker Bay, Lily White) Bazzill Basics Paper *Rubber stamp:* (1957 Bel Air) Cornish Heritage Farms *Dye ink:* (Pale Violet, Brilliant Yellow, Pine Green) Marvy Uchida *Pigment ink:* (blue) Stampabilities *Font:* (Calibri) Microsoft *Tools:* (1", 1¼", 1¾" circle punches) EK Success

**SUPPLIES:** *Cardstock:* (Shamrock) Core'dinations; (KI White) Bazzill Basics Paper *Patterned paper:* (Sophie Anne Summer Fields from Penny Lane collection) My Mind's Eye *Clear stamps:* (flowers from Dot Spot set; birthday wishes from Asian Fusion set) Papertrey Ink *Pigment ink:* (Marigold, Royal Blue) Clearsnap *Chalk ink:* (Warm Violet) Clearsnap *Accents:* (blue rhinestones) Doodlebug Design; (green rhinestones) Glitz Design *Fibers:* (yellow polka dot ribbon) Renaissance By Design *Die:* (scallop) Papertrey Ink

## :5: Peacock Celebration

Designer: Kim Hughes

❶ Make card from cardstock. ❷ Die-cut feather from cardstock; adhere. ❸ Apply rub-on. ❹ Adhere cardstock strips; round bottom corners of front flap. ❺ Stitch edges, adhere button, and tie on twill.

*Finished size: 2¾" x 6"*

## :5: Enjoy

Designer: Teri Anderson

❶ Make card from cardstock. ❷ Adhere cardstock strips and patterned paper panel. ❸ Die-cut flourishes from cardstock; adhere. ❹ Stamp enjoy on cardstock strip; mat with cardstock and adhere. ❺ Adhere rhinestones.

*Finished size: 4¼" x 5½"*

**SUPPLIES:** *Cardstock:* (Jubilee, Shamrock, Breaker Bay, Marigold) Bazzill Basics Paper *Accent:* (orange button) Papertrey Ink *Rub-on:* (celebrate) Making Memories *Fibers:* (blue twill) Papertrey Ink *Die:* (feather) Provo Craft *Tool:* (corner rounder punch) Fiskars

**SUPPLIES:** *Cardstock:* (Jubilee, Shamrock, Breaker Bay, Desert Marigold) Bazzill Basics Paper; (white) Georgia-Pacific *Patterned paper:* (Dandelions from Fly a Kite collection) October Afternoon *Clear stamps:* (enjoy from Spiral Bouquet set) Papertrey Ink *Specialty ink:* (Enchanted Evening hybrid) Papertrey Ink *Accents:* (green rhinestones) Kaisercraft *Die:* (flourish) Provo Craft

PATTERN

Find the pattern for making Kim Hughes's Thank You Teacher card on p.192.

## Deepest Sympathy

Designer: Lea Lawson

❶ Make card from cardstock. Adhere patterned paper; round bottom corners. ❷ Adhere cardstock panel; stamp sentiment. ❸ Border-punch cardstock strip and adhere. ❹ Tie on ribbon. Adhere leaves. ❺ Stamp flower on cardstock; emboss. Trim and adhere. ❻ Adhere rhinestones and button.

*Finished size: 5½" x 4¼"*

## Thank You Teacher

Designer: Kim Hughes

❶ Make card from cardstock; round bottom corners. Stamp sentiment. ❷ Cut apple from cardstock, following pattern; stamp stars and adhere. ❸ Trim cardstock into stem and adhere. ❹ Stamp ruler on cardstock. Trim into leaf and adhere. ❺ Thread buttons with floss and adhere.

*Finished size: 4" x 5½"*

**SUPPLIES:** *Cardstock:* (Forest, Windy, Razzleberry Dark) Bazzill Basics Paper *Patterned paper:* (Red Medium Polka Dots from Lush collection) My Mind's Eye *Clear stamps:* (flower from Year of Flowers: Violets set, sentiment from Asian Fusion set) Papertrey Ink *Pigment ink:* (Evergreen) Clearsnap *Watermark ink:* Clearsnap *Embossing powder:* (Liquid Platinum) Ranger Industries *Accents:* (green felt leaves) Provo Craft; (red rhinestones) Creative Imaginations; (red button) Papertrey Ink *Fibers:* (gray ribbon) Michaels *Tools:* (corner rounder punch) EK Success; (border punch) Fiskars

**SUPPLIES:** *Cardstock:* (Windy, Blush Red Dark, Forest, Razzleberry Dark) Bazzill Basics Paper *Rubber stamps:* (sentiment, ruler, stars from Fhiona's School House set) Your Next Stamp *Pigment ink:* (Vintage Cream) Papertrey Ink *Solvent ink:* (Olive Green) Tsukineko *Specialty ink:* (Scarlet Jewel hybrid) Papertrey Ink *Accents:* (gray buttons) SEI *Fibers:* (gray floss) DMC *Tool:* (corner rounder punch) Fiskars

## Lovely Birthday

Designer: Latisha Yoast

**①** Make card from cardstock. **②** Punch top edge of cardstock panel; adhere patterned paper and cardstock strips. Border-punch cardstock strip and adhere. **③** Stamp birthday wishes on panel. Tie on ribbon. **④** Adhere with foam tape.

*Finished size: 4" x 4½"*

## Get Well Hugs & Wishes

Designer: Chan Vuong

**①** Make card from cardstock. Cover with patterned paper and round one corner. **②** Stamp sentiment on cardstock strip. Score and border-punch; adhere. **③** Adhere butterfly with foam tape. **④** Adhere buttons and attach clip.

*Finished size: 5" x 4¼"*

**SUPPLIES:** *Cardstock:* (Windy, Blissful embossed, Razzleberry Dark) Bazzill Basics Paper *Patterned paper:* (Woolens from Mitten Weather collection) Cosmo Cricket *Clear stamp:* (birthday wishes from Fancy Phrases set) Waltzingmouse Stamps *Dye ink:* (Tuxedo Black) Tsukineko *Fibers:* (green ribbon) Papertrey Ink *Tool:* (border punch) Fiskars

**SUPPLIES:** *Cardstock:* (white) Papertrey Ink; (kraft) *Patterned paper:* (gray floral from Madeline pad) SEI *Clear stamp:* (sentiment from Big & Bold Wishes set) Papertrey Ink *Pigment ink:* (Onyx Black) Tsukineko *Accents:* (white library clip) Stampin' Up!; (clear, red, green buttons) *Sticker:* (butterfly) Echo Park Paper *Tools:* (corner rounder punch) Fiskars; (border punch) EK Success

## Love You

Designer: Kalyn Kepner

① Make card from cardstock; emboss. ② Adhere patterned paper and cardstock strips. ③ Stitch border. ④ Thread buttons with floss and adhere. ⑤ Stamp love you on sticker and adhere with foam tape.

*Finished size: 5½" x 4¼"*

## So Sweet

Designer: Lea Lawson

① Make card from cardstock; round bottom corners. ② Round bottom corners of cardstock panel. ③ Stamp borders and sentiment on panel. Adhere ribbon around panel. Tie ribbon bow and adhere. ④ Adhere panel. ⑤ Stamp daffodils on patterned paper and cardstock. Trim and adhere with foam tape. ⑥ Adhere pearls.

*Finished size: 4¼" x 5½"*

**SUPPLIES:** *Cardstock:* (Velvet, Candle, Blush Red Dark, Lily White) Bazzill Basics Paper *Patterned paper:* (Still in Box from The Thrift Shop collection) October Afternoon *Clear stamp:* (love you from Series 41 set) Studio G *Chalk ink:* (Lipstick Red) Clearsnap *Accents:* (burgundy buttons) Papertrey Ink *Sticker:* (label) October Afternoon *Fibers:* (burgundy floss) DMC *Template:* (embossing Swiss Dots) Provo Craft

**SUPPLIES:** *Cardstock:* (Velvet, Candle, Lily White) Bazzill Basics Paper *Patterned paper:* (Swiss Dot from Ladybug Boutique collection) Doodlebug Design *Clear stamps:* (dotted, solid diamond borders from A Little Argyle set; daffodils from Year of Flowers: Daffodils set; sentiment from Year of Flowers: Sweet Peas set) Papertrey Ink *Pigment ink:* (Eggplant, Cranberry) Clearsnap; (Onyx Black) Tsukineko *Accents:* (gold, red pearls) Kaisercraft *Fibers:* (purple ribbon) *Tool:* (corner rounder punch) EK Success

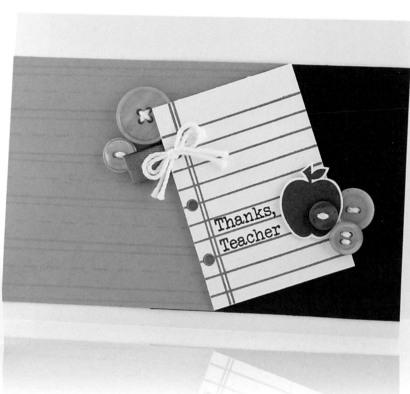

## ⑤ Thanks So Much Owl

Designer: Laura O'Donnell

❶ Make card from cardstock. ❷ Punch bottom edge of cardstock panel and adhere. ❸ Stamp owl twice on cardstock. Color images. Adhere one image to card. ❹ Cut out owl and frame from second image; adhere with foam tape. ❺ Adhere rhinestone.

*Finished size: 3¾" x 5"*

## Thanks, Teacher

Designer: Maile Belles

❶ Make card from cardstock. ❷ Stamp alphabet and lined backgrounds on cardstock. Trim and adhere. ❸ Stamp paper sheet and thanks, teacher on cardstock. Cut out and punch holes. ❹ Adhere twill loop behind stamped piece; adhere to card with foam tape. ❺ Stamp apple on cardstock. Cut out and adhere with foam tape. ❻ Thread buttons with yarn and adhere. Tie yarn bow and adhere.

*Finished size: 5½" x 4¼"*

**SUPPLIES:** *Cardstock:* (Velvet) Bazzill Basics Paper; (white) Neenah Paper *Rubber stamps:* (Thanks So Much Owl) Hero Arts *Dye ink:* (Tuxedo Black) Tsukineko *Color medium:* (assorted markers) Copic *Accent:* (purple rhinestone) Queen & Co. *Tool:* (border punch) Fiskars

**SUPPLIES:** All supplies from Papertrey Ink unless otherwise noted. *Cardstock:* (Summer Sunrise, white); (red) Bazzill Basics Paper *Clear stamps:* (apple; paper sheet; alphabet background; lined background; thanks, teacher from School Time set) *Pigment ink:* (Plum Pudding) *Watermark ink:* Tsukineko *Specialty ink:* (Pure Poppy, True Black hybrid) *Accents:* (orange, purple buttons) *Fibers:* (purple twill); (white yarn) no source *Tool:* (⅛" circle punch) Fiskars

## Brighten My Day

Designer: Melanie Douthit

1 Make card from cardstock. 2 Emboss cardstock panel. Round corners and adhere. 3 Round bottom corners of patterned paper strip; adhere. 4 Punch bottom edge of cardstock strip; adhere. 5 Adhere rickrack, flowers, and buttons. Affix sticker.

*Finished size: 5" square*

## Thanks Sew Much

Designer: Betsy Veldman

1 Make card from cardstock. 2 Stamp flourished circle, medallion, half circle loops, and flower repeatedly on cardstock panel, forming doilies. Stitch and ink edges. 3 Adhere patterned paper, lace, and die cut paper strips. Zigzag-stitch top edge. 4 Adhere tag. Tie ribbon on stick pin and attach. 5 Thread buttons with floss and adhere. 6 Spell "Thanks" and "Sew much" with stickers. Adhere panel to card.

*Finished size: 4½" x 4¾"*

**SUPPLIES:** *Cardstock:* (Sunshine, Razzleberry Dark, Papaya Puree Dark) Bazzill Basics Paper *Patterned paper:* (Orange Pink Wash from Pocket Full of Posies pad) DCWV Inc. *Accents:* (pink flowers, buttons) Imaginisce *Sticker:* (sentiment) BasicGrey *Fibers:* (pink rickrack) Northern Threads *Template:* (embossing Stylized Flowers) Provo Craft *Tools:* (border punch) Fiskars; (corner rounder punch) Creative Memories

**SUPPLIES:** *Cardstock:* (Rustic Cream) Papertrey Ink *Patterned paper:* (pink floral from Razzleberry Lemonade collection) Stampin' Up!; (Measuring Up from Material Girl collection) Cosmo Cricket *Specialty paper:* (Plum Doily die cut from Indian Summer collection) BasicGrey *Clear stamps:* (flourished circle from Spooky Sweets II set; medallion from Giga Guide Lines set; half circle loops from Mini Scrapbook Series: Tabs set; flower from Borders and Corners {Circle} set) Papertrey Ink *Pigment ink:* (Orange Zest, Hibiscus Burst) Papertrey Ink *Chalk ink:* (Creamy Brown) Clearsnap *Specialty ink:* (Scarlet Jewel, Summer Sunrise hybrid) Papertrey Ink *Accents:* (pink, cream, burgundy buttons) Papertrey Ink; (pink flower stick pin) Little Yellow Bicycle; (cream tag) 7gypsies *Stickers:* (Mini alphabet) My Little Shoebox; (Sultry alphabet) BasicGrey *Fibers:* (yellow gingham ribbon) May Arts; (orange floss) DMC; (orange vintage lace)

## Full of Fleur-de-Lis

Designer: Alison Anderson

① Make card from cardstock. ② Punch fleurs-de-lis from cardstock; adhere. ③ Stamp merci on cardstock. Punch into circle and mat with punched cardstock circle; adhere. ④ Tie on ribbon.

*Finished size: 4¼" x 5½"*

## Colorful Get Well

Designer: Jessica Witty

① Make card from cardstock. ② Cover cardstock panel with patterned paper strips; adhere felt. Zigzag-stitch seams. ③ Ink edges. Tie on ribbon. ④ Stamp get well on patterned paper; punch into tag. Attach with pin. ⑤ Adhere panel with foam tape.

*Finished size: 3½" x 5"*

**SUPPLIES:** *Cardstock:* (Hot Pink, Sunshine, Papaya Puree Dark, Razzleberry Dark) Bazzill Basics Paper *Rubber stamp:* (Merci) Stampabilities *Solvent ink:* (black) Tsukineko *Fibers:* (yellow ribbon) Schiff Ribbons *Tools:* (fleur-de-lis punch) Martha Stewart Crafts; (1½", 1¾" circle punches) Stampin' Up!

**SUPPLIES:** *Cardstock:* (Razzleberry Dark) Bazzill Basics Paper; (Summer Sunrise) Papertrey Ink *Patterned paper:* (Sugar on Top from Sweet Shoppe collection) Collage Press; (Picnic Table, Dandelions from Fly a Kite collection) October Afternoon; (Cornbread from Nook & Pantry collection) BasicGrey; (pink swirl) *Clear stamp:* (get well from Mega Mixed Messages set) Papertrey Ink *Dye ink:* (Chamomile) Papertrey Ink *Pigment ink:* (Dark Peony) Clearsnap *Accent:* (copper pin) Making Memories *Fibers:* (yellow ribbon) Papertrey Ink *Tool:* (tag punch) Martha Stewart Crafts *Other:* (pink felt) Kunin Felt

## Happy Birthday to You

Designer: Lisa Johnson

❶ Make card from cardstock. ❷ Cut cardstock strips. Stamp script on one strip and adhere strips. ❸ Die-cut border from cardstock; adhere. ❹ Adhere ribbon. ❺ Thread buttons with twine; adhere. ❻ Stamp sentiment and you on cardstock; punch into rectangle. Die-cut border from cardstock; adhere. Adhere piece with foam tape.

*Finished size: 4¼" square*

## Sew Sweet

Designer: Julie Campbell

❶ Make card from cardstock. ❷ Stamp sew sweet on cardstock panel. Mat with cardstock. ❸ Adhere felt. Zigzag-stitch three edges. Ink edges of doily and adhere. ❹ Trim patterned paper and adhere. Die-cut scallops from cardstock; adhere. ❺ Stamp button card on cardstock. Cut out, ink edges, and adhere. ❻ Thread buttons with crochet thread and adhere. Adhere trim. Adhere panel.

*Finished size: 4¼" x 5½"*

**SUPPLIES:** *Cardstock:* (Pansy, Sweetheart) Bazzill Basics Paper; (white) Papertrey Ink *Clear stamps:* (sentiment, you from All About You set; script from Background Basics: Text Style II set) Papertrey Ink *Dye ink:* (Eggplant Envy) Stampin' Up! *Specialty ink:* (Landscape hybrid) Stewart Superior Corp. *Accents:* (white buttons) Papertrey Ink *Fibers:* (green leaf ribbon) Papertrey Ink; (cream twine) *Die:* (scalloped border) Papertrey Ink *Tool:* (rectangle punch) Marvy Uchida

**SUPPLIES:** *Cardstock:* (Majestic Purple Dark) Prism; (Parakeet) Bazzill Basics Paper; (white) Papertrey Ink *Patterned paper:* (Last One from The Thrift Shop collection) October Afternoon *Rubber stamps:* (button card from LeChic set; sew sweet from Material Girl set) Unity Stamp Co. *Dye ink:* (Chai, Chamomile) Papertrey Ink *Chalk ink:* (Dark Brown) Clearsnap *Accents:* (green, pink buttons) Papertrey Ink, Autumn Leaves; (white doily) Wilton *Fibers:* (green flower trim) Webster's Pages; (white crochet thread) *Die:* (scallops) My Favorite Things *Other:* (pink felt) Heather Bailey

## Just Because Collage

*Designer: Vanessa Menhorn*

❶ Make card from cardstock. ❷ Die-cut label and square from patterned paper; trim and adhere. ❸ Die-cut rectangle, square, and flower from cardstock; adhere. ❹ Punch butterfly from patterned paper; adhere. ❺ Adhere ribbon, pearls, and rhinestones. ❻ Thread button with floss and adhere. ❼ Stamp sentiment.

*Finished size: 5½" x 4¼"*

## ⑤Floral Feel Better Soon

*Designer: Lea Lawson*

❶ Make card from cardstock; round bottom corners. ❷ Stamp flowers and sentiment on cardstock panel; adhere. ❸ Stamp flowers on patterned paper; emboss. Cut out and adhere. ❹ Tie on ribbon. Thread button with twine and adhere. ❺ Adhere rhinestones. Apply glitter glue.

*Finished size: 4¼" x 5½"*

**SUPPLIES:** *Cardstock:* (Parakeet, Pansy) Bazzill Basics Paper; (white) *Patterned paper:* (Front Porch, Gazebo, purple/black flourish from Bayberry Cottage collection) Pink Paislee *Clear stamps:* (just because from Damask Designs set) Papertrey Ink *Pigment ink:* (Graphite Black) Tsukineko *Accents:* (pink pearls) Prima; (purple button) Papertrey Ink; (green rhinestones) Hero Arts *Fibers:* (purple pleated ribbon) Pink Paislee; (white floss) *Dies:* (rectangle, squares, label) Spellbinders; (flower) Provo Craft *Tool:* (butterfly punch) Martha Stewart Crafts

**SUPPLIES:** *Cardstock:* (Sweetheart, Lily White) Bazzill Basics Paper *Patterned paper:* (Concord Dot from Double Dot collection) BoBunny Press *Clear stamps:* (flowers from Year of Flowers: Gladiolus set; sentiment from Asian Fusion set) Papertrey Ink *Pigment ink:* (Moss Green, black) Clearsnap *Embossing powder:* (white) BasicGrey *Accents:* (pink button) BasicGrey; (iridescent glitter glue) Ranger Industries; (pink, purple rhinestones) *Fibers:* (green ribbon) Papertrey Ink; (natural twine) Darice *Tool:* (corner rounder punch) EK Success

**BONUS IDEA**

With a different sentiment, the design and color scheme of this card could easily fit a sympathy occasion.

## Butterfly Wishes

Designer: Kalyn Kepner

① Make card from cardstock. ② Stamp sentiment; emboss. ③ Trim vellum and tie on ribbon; mat with cardstock. Adhere; adhere rhinestones. ④ Stamp butterflies on cardstock; emboss two. Trim and adhere with foam tape.

*Finished size: 5½" x 3½"*

## Fabulous Day

Designer: Maile Belles

① Make card from cardstock. ② Trim patterned paper and adhere. ③ Stamp Chandelier on cardstock; emboss. Trim and adhere with foam tape. ④ Stamp sentiment. Adhere rhinestones.

*Finished size: 4¼" x 5½"*

**SUPPLIES:** *Cardstock:* (Emperor metallic, Platinum metallic, Lily White) Bazzill Basics Paper *Vellum:* (White Swirls Gold Dust) Paper Source *Clear stamps:* (birthday wishes from Tea for Two Additions set) Papertrey Ink; (butterflies from Butterfly Collector set) Layers of Color *Watermark ink:* Tsukineko *Chalk ink:* (Wisteria) Clearsnap *Embossing powder:* (silver, gold, white) Hampton Art *Accents:* (purple rhinestones) Queen & Co. *Fibers:* (gold ribbon) Paper Source

**SUPPLIES:** *Cardstock:* (Purple Shimmer) DCWV Inc. *Patterned paper:* (silver Mini Chandeliers) Hambly Screen Prints *Rubber stamp:* (Chandelier) Hero Arts *Watermark ink:* Tsukineko *Specialty ink:* (Noir hybrid) Stewart Superior Corp. *Embossing powder:* (gold glitter) American Crafts *Accents:* (purple rhinestones) Kaisercraft

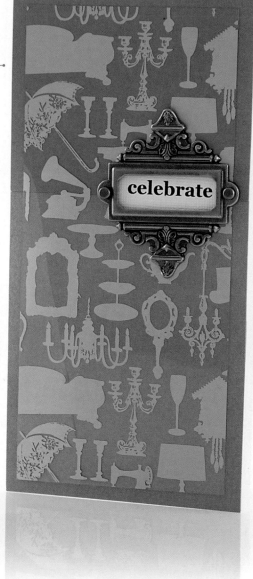

## DESIGNER TIP
Apply adhesive beneath patterned images on a transparency to keep adhesive from showing.

## Wishing You Comfort
Designer: Tiffany Johnson

① Make card from cardstock; round one corner. ② Stamp flowers and stems on cardstock; trim, round one corner, and adhere. Adhere pearls. ③ Stamp sentiment on cardstock; punch edge. Trim and adhere.

*Finished size: 4¼" x 5"*

## Metallic Celebrate
Designer: Julia Stainton

① Make card from cardstock. ② Trim cardstock and adhere. ③ Trim transparency sheet and adhere. ④ Print celebrate on cardstock; trim and adhere. ⑤ Adhere book plate.

*Finished size: 4¼" x 5½"*

**SUPPLIES:** *Cardstock:* (Gold Leaf metallic) Bazzill Basics Paper; (silver metallic) Hambly Screen Prints; (Solar White) Neenah Paper *Rubber stamps:* (sentiment, flowers, stem from Many Wishes set) Gina K Designs *Dye ink:* (Rich Cocoa) Tsukineko *Chalk ink:* (Wisteria) Clearsnap *Accents:* (purple pearls) Prima *Tools:* (corner rounder punch) EK Success; (border punch) Fiskars

**SUPPLIES:** *Cardstock:* (Gold Leaf metallic, Emperor metallic, Snow) Bazzill Basics Paper *Transparency sheet:* (silver Home Decor) Hambly Screen Prints *Accent:* (silver book plate) Tim Holtz *Font:* (Georgia) www.fonts.com

## Metallic Congratulations

Designer: Beth Opel

❶ Make card from cardstock. ❷ Trim and score cardstock; adhere. Tie on ribbon. ❸ Print "Congratulations" on cardstock. Die-cut and emboss into label. Die-cut and emboss label from patterned paper, trim, and adhere to sentiment label. ❹ Die-cut and emboss label from cardstock. Mat sentiment label with cardstock label, using foam tape. ❺ Adhere label with foam tape. ❻ Adhere copper leaf and beads; attach pin.

*Finished size: 5½" x 4¼"*

## Out of This World

Designer: Maren Benedict

❶ Make card from cardstock. ❷ Die-cut and emboss circle from cardstock; stamp earth in orbit. Stamp image on cardstock, cut pieces, and adhere to circle. Adhere circle to card with foam tape. ❸ Punch circles from cardstock and adhere in layers. ❹ Stamp sentiment on cardstock; trim and attach brad. Adhere with foam tape. ❺ Tie on ribbon.

*Finished size: 4¼" x 5½"*

**SUPPLIES:** *Cardstock:* (Copper metallic, Gold Leaf metallic, ivory) Bazzill Basics Paper *Patterned paper:* (Rosice from Moravia collection) SEI *Accents:* (copper metallic leaf, brown beads) Making Memories; (cream flower stick pin) Little Yellow Bicycle *Fibers:* (teal ribbon) American Crafts *Font:* (Freebooter Script) www.dafont.com *Dies:* (labels) Spellbinders *Tool:* (scoring board) Martha Stewart Crafts

**SUPPLIES:** *Cardstock:* (Copper metallic, Emerald metallic, Gold Leaf metallic) Bazzill Basics Paper *Rubber stamps:* (sentiment, earth in orbit from Out of This World set) Unity Stamp Co. *Dye ink:* (Tuxedo Black) Tsukineko *Accent:* (copper brad) American Crafts *Fibers:* (gold ribbon) Martha Stewart Crafts *Die:* (circle) Spellbinders *Tool:* (circle punch) Stampin' Up!

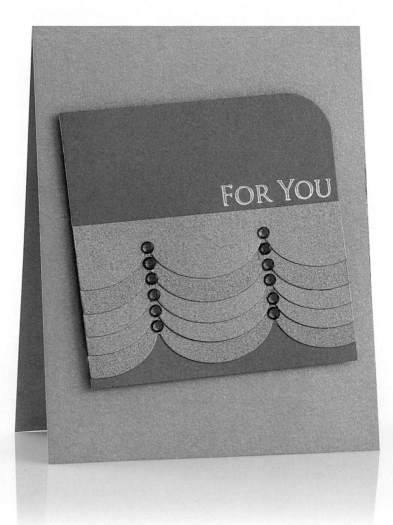

## Metallic For You

Designer: Tiffany Johnson

❶ Make card from cardstock. ❷ Stamp for you on cardstock; trim and round one corner. Adhere with foam tape. ❸ Die-cut border strips from cardstock; trim and adhere. ❹ Adhere rhinestones.

*Finished size: 4¼" x 5½"*

## Birthday Flowers

Designer: Kim Kesti

❶ Make card from cardstock; round right corners. ❷ Trim patterned paper; adhere. Trim cardstock strip and adhere. ❸ Fussy-cut flowers from patterned paper; attach brads. Adhere with foam tape. ❹ Affix sticker.

*Finished size: 4¼" x 5"*

**SUPPLIES:** *Cardstock:* (Copper metallic, Emerald metallic, Gold Leaf metallic) Bazzill Basics Paper *Clear stamp:* (for you from Little Box Labels set) Waltzingmouse Stamps *Pigment ink:* (white) Clearsnap *Accents:* (orange rhinestones) Hero Arts *Die:* (scallop border) My Favorite Things *Tool:* (corner rounder punch) EK Success

**SUPPLIES:** *Cardstock:* (Copper metallic, Emerald metallic) Bazzill Basics Paper *Patterned paper:* (Eleanor from Botanique collection) American Crafts *Accents:* (gold brads) Office Max *Sticker:* (sentiment) SRM Press *Tool:* (corner rounder punch) W R Memory Keepers

DESIGNER TIP
Heat setting is a must when stamping with pigment ink on metallic paper. Without it, the ink may smear.

## ⦂5⦂ Celebrate with Cake

Designer: Winter Sims

❶ Make card from cardstock. ❷ Stamp celebrate. ❸ Tie on ribbon. ❹ Adhere sticker with foam tape.

*Finished size: 5½" x 4¼"*

## ⦂5⦂ Baby Shower

Designer: Lisa Johnson

❶ Make card from cardstock. ❷ Stamp umbrella handle and sentiment on cardstock panel; heat set. (See Designer Tip.) ❸ Stamp umbrella top on cardstock; heat set, fussy-cut, and adhere to panel with foam tape. ❹ Die-cut cardstock border; adhere. ❺ Adhere panel to card. Tie on ribbon.

*Finished size: 4¼" x 5½"*

**SUPPLIES:** *Cardstock:* (Pinkini) Bazzill Basics Paper *Clear stamp:* (celebrate from Damask Designs set) Papertrey Ink *Pigment ink:* (gold) Clearsnap *Sticker:* (wedding cake) EK Success *Fibers:* (gold ribbon) Hobby Lobby

**SUPPLIES:** *Cardstock:* (Gold Leaf metallic, Satin Wedding White shimmer, Pinkini) Bazzill Basics Paper *Clear stamps:* (umbrella, handle from Scattered Showers set; sentiment from Baby Button Bits set) Papertrey Ink *Pigment ink:* (Gold) Tsukineko *Fibers:* (white ribbon) Papertrey Ink *Die:* (scallop border) Papertrey Ink

DESIGNER TIP

For the best adhesion, use a liquid glue to secure chipboard.

## :5: Happily Ever After

Designer: Lisa Johnson

❶ Make card from cardstock. ❷ Stamp sentiment on cardstock panel; heat set. ❸ Round left corners of panel; adhere ribbon and adhere with foam tape. ❹ Adhere swirl.

*Finished size: 5½" x 4¼"*

## :5: Pink & Gold Congratulations

Designer: Windy Robinson

❶ Make card from cardstock. ❷ Emboss cardstock panel; mat with cardstock. Adhere rhinestones. ❸ Die-cut label from cardstock and adhere to panel with foam tape. ❹ Tie ribbon around panel; adhere panel to card. ❺ Stamp congratulations on cardstock; trim into tag and adhere with foam tape.

*Finished size: 4¼" x 5½"*

**SUPPLIES:** *Cardstock:* (Gold Leaf metallic, Satin Wedding White shimmer) Bazzill Basics Paper *Clear stamps:* (Mr. & Mrs., sentiment from Big & Bold Wishes set) Papertrey Ink *Pigment ink:* (Gold) Tsukineko *Accent:* (pink glitter chipboard swirl) Pebbles *Fibers:* (gold ribbon) Papertrey Ink *Tool:* (corner rounder punch) EK Success

**SUPPLIES:** *Cardstock:* (Gold Leaf metallic, Satin Wedding White shimmer, Pinkini) Bazzill Basics Paper *Clear stamps:* (congratulations from Strictly Sentiments set) Renaissance by Design *Pigment ink:* (Vintage Sepia) Tsukineko *Accents:* (gold rhinestones) Zva Creative *Fibers:* (gold ribbon) May Arts *Template:* (embossing argyle) QuicKutz *Die:* (label) QuicKutz

DESIGNER TIPS

Use a piercing template or ruler to get evenly spaced holes for a row of brads.

Don't be afraid to cut away portions of pre-made rub-ons if they don't work with your design.

DESIGNER TIP

Add energy to your cards by combining interesting finishes. Glittery gold and silver against a shiny, smooth transparency makes for an exciting design partnership.

## Love-ly Hearts

Designer: Jessica Witty

1 Make card from cardstock. 2 Trim transparency sheet into overlay and adhere. 3 Punch hearts from cardstock; adhere, using foam tape for gold hearts. 4 Stamp love you on vellum and trim into flag. Attach with pin.

*Finished size: 3½" x 4¼"*

## Elegant Best Wishes

Designer: Julia Stainton

1 Make card from cardstock; round bottom corners. 2 Trim patterned paper; adhere. 3 Trim cardstock; adhere. Attach brads, inserting one through flower. 4 Apply rub-on.

*Finished size: 4" x 6"*

**SUPPLIES:** *Cardstock:* (white) Papertrey Ink; (silver, gold glitter) Best Creations *Vellum:* Stampin' Up! *Transparency sheet:* Office Depot *Clear stamp:* (love you from Daily Designs Sentiments set) Papertrey Ink *Pigment ink:* (gold) Clearsnap *Accent:* (clear stick pin) Maya Road *Tool:* (heart punch) EK Success

**SUPPLIES:** *Cardstock:* (Gold Leaf metallic, Bazzill White) Bazzill Basics Paper *Patterned paper:* (silver Patchwork) Hambly Screen Prints *Accents:* (white flower) Prima; (silver brads) Making Memories *Rub-on:* (best wishes) BasicGrey *Tool:* (corner rounder punch) EK Success

DESIGNER TIP
Notice how the placement of the bee flying up coordinates with the card's sentiment.

## Hostess Thanks

Designer: Tiffany Johnson

❶ Make card from cardstock. ❷ Trim patterned paper and adhere. ❸ Die-cut and emboss oval from cardstock. ❹ Stamp thanks on oval; emboss. Apply rub-on and adhere with foam tape. ❺ Adhere pearls.

*Finished size: 4¼" x 5½"*

## Hopeful Bee

Designer: Beth Opel

❶ Make card from cardstock. ❷ Trim cardstock and adhere with foam tape. ❸ Trim bee image from patterned paper and adhere to frame. Adhere frame to card. ❹ Print sentiment on cardstock. Trim and mount on cardstock panel. Adhere ribbon. Tie ribbon bow and adhere. ❺ Adhere panel to card with foam tape.

*Finished size: 3½" x 6"*

**SUPPLIES:** *Cardstock:* (Solar White) Neenah Paper; (Gold Leaf metallic) Bazzill Basics Paper *Patterned paper:* (gold Antique Doily) Hambly Screen Prints *Clear stamp:* (thanks from Say It in Style set) Close To My Heart *Pigment ink:* (Fresh Snow) Papertrey Ink *Embossing powder:* (white) Stampendous! *Accents:* (silver pearls) *Rub-on:* (silverware) Hambly Screen Prints *Die:* (oval) Spellbinders

**SUPPLIES:** *Cardstock:* (white) American Crafts; (silver) DCWV Inc. *Patterned paper:* (Metallique Specialty Bees Shimmer from Paper Reverie collection) Making Memories *Sticker:* (gold glitter chipboard frame) American Crafts *Fibers:* (gold ribbon) Little Yellow Bicycle *Fonts:* (AL Fantasy Type) www.fonts101.com; (Garamond) www.fonts.com

**DESIGNER TIPS**

When adding multiple paper layers, trim card edge with a guillotine-style paper trimmer for a crisp edge.

When placing rhinestone flourishes on your card, cut half the backing off, place where desired, and then apply the other half. This keeps the rhinestones from skewing and sticking to your fingers.

## Red Birthday Wishes

Designer: Chan Vuong

❶ Make card from cardstock; score right side. ❷ Stamp flower burst borders and birthday wishes. ❸ Trim cardstock strip; adhere. ❹ Die-cut flower from cardstock and curl petals; adhere. Punch circle from patterned paper and adhere with foam tape.

*Finished size: 4" x 3¼"*

## You Make My Heart Happy

Designer: Julia Stainton

❶ Make card from cardstock. ❷ Adhere patterned paper and cardstock strips. Adhere trim. ❸ Adhere rhinestones and insert pins. ❹ Stamp sentiment.

*Finished size: 4¼" x 5½"*

**SUPPLIES:** *Cardstock:* (white) Papertrey Ink; (red shimmer) DCWV Inc. *Patterned paper:* (red polka dot from Craft Fair pad) American Crafts *Clear stamps:* (flower burst border from Song Writers set) Sassafras Lass; (birthday wishes from Up, Up & Away set) Papertrey Ink *Pigment ink:* (Crimson Red) Tsukineko *Die:* (flower) Stampin' Up! *Tool:* (circle punch) EK Success

**SUPPLIES:** *Cardstock:* (Watermelon, Maraschino, Pomegranate) Bazzill Basics Paper *Patterned paper:* (Story Hour from Report Card pad) October Afternoon *Clear stamp:* (sentiment from Anytime Messages set) Hero Arts *Dye ink:* (Jet Black reinker) Ranger Industries *Accents:* (red heart pins) Maya Road; (clear rhinestone flourishes) Zva Creative *Fibers:* (red flower trim) Webster's Pages

### Three Red Flowers

Designer: Kim Kesti

1 Make card from cardstock. 2 Wrap ribbon around card front; adhere. 3 Stamp flower on cardstock; round corners. Attach brads and mat with cardstock. 4 Trim patterned paper with border punch and adhere to block. 5 Apply rub-on. Adhere block to card with foam tape.

*Finished size: 4¾" x 3¼"*

### I Just Love You

Designer: Kelley Eubanks

1 Make card from cardstock; round bottom corners. 2 Stamp sentiment and emboss. 3 Adhere rhinestone. 4 Punch hearts from cardstock; adhere to twine. 5 Adhere heart strings to card.

*Finished size: 4¼" x 5½"*

**SUPPLIES:** *Cardstock:* (Watermelon, Maraschino, Pomegranate, Lily White) Bazzill Basics Paper *Patterned paper:* (Melody from Tree House collection) Pebbles *Clear stamp:* (flower from Funky Flowers set) My Stamp Box *Dye ink:* (Real Red) Stampin' Up! *Accents:* (red brads) Pebbles *Rub-on:* (thank you) Pebbles *Fibers:* (red stitched ribbon) Pebbles *Tool:* (border punch)

**SUPPLIES:** *Cardstock:* (Watermelon, Maraschino, Pomegranate) Bazzill Basics Paper *Clear stamps:* (sentiment from Loving Words set) Technique Tuesday *Watermark ink:* Tsukineko *Embossing powder:* (clear) Stewart Superior Corp. *Accent:* (red rhinestone) My Mind's Eye *Fibers:* (red/white twine) Shabby Green Door *Tools:* (small heart punch, corner rounder punch) Stampin' Up!

**DESIGNER TIP**
Arrange monochromatic tones
from darkest to lightest for a
subtle variegated look.

**DESIGNER TIP**
Keep sympathy cards soft and
subtle for a soothing look.

### 5 STEPS With Sympathy

Designer: Julia Stainton

❶ Make card from cardstock. ❷ Cut cardstock square, mat with cardstock, and adhere. ❸ Apply rub-on. ❹ Tie twine on pin; adhere pins. Affix badge.

*Finished size: 4¼" square*

### 5 STEPS Rustic Orange Note

Designer: Julia Stainton

❶ Make card from cardstock. ❷ Trim cardstock pieces; distress bottom edges, layer, and adhere. Ink card edges. ❸ Adhere rhinestone swirls. Tie twine bow and adhere. Adhere flower.

*Finished size: 4" x 5½"*

**SUPPLIES:** *Cardstock:* (Cantaloupe, Apricot, Yam) Bazzill Basics Paper *Accents:* (copper leaf pins) Maya Road *Rub-on:* (with sympathy) American Crafts *Sticker:* (flourish badge) American Crafts *Fibers:* (natural jute twine) Westrim Crafts

**SUPPLIES:** *Cardstock:* (Cantaloupe, Apricot, Yam) Bazzill Basics Paper *Dye ink:* (Brushed Corduroy) Ranger Industries *Accents:* (burlap flower) Prima; (brown, clear rhinestone swirls) Zva Creative *Fibers:* (natural jute twine) Westrim Crafts

## Orange Blooming Hello

Designer: Kelley Eubanks

❶ Make card from cardstock; round bottom corners. ❷ Stamp flower on each cardstock, cut out, and adhere pieces to card with foam tape. Apply glitter glue. ❸ Stamp hello.

*Finished size: 4" square*

## 4 Ever Birdie Friends

Designer: Kim Kesti

❶ Make card from cardstock. ❷ Trim cardstock slightly smaller than card front; adhere. ❸ Trim die cut paper; adhere. ❹ Apply rub-on to tag. Affix chipboard birds and tie on ribbon. Thread button with twine and adhere. ❺ Trim heart from cardstock, ink edges, and adhere to tag. ❻ Adhere tag to card with foam tape.

*Finished size: 4¼" x 6½"*

**SUPPLIES:** *Cardstock:* (Cantaloupe, Apricot, Yam) Bazzill Basics Paper *Clear stamps:* (flower from In Bloom set) Papertrey Ink; (hello from Essential Messages set) Hero Arts *Dye ink:* (Tuxedo Black) Tsukineko *Accent:* (white glitter glue) Ranger Industries *Tools:* (corner rounder punch) Stampin' Up!

**SUPPLIES:** *Cardstock:* (Cantaloupe, Apricot) Bazzill Basics Paper *Specialty paper:* (Decorative die cut from Unwritten collection) Reminisce *Chalk ink:* (Amber Clay) Clearsnap *Accents:* (orange button) BasicGrey; (shipping tag) Office Max *Rub-on:* (sentiment) Melissa Frances *Stickers:* (chipboard birds) Cosmo Cricket *Fibers:* (peach ribbon) Offray; (natural hemp twine)

**DESIGNER TIP**
Foam alphabet stickers are easily colored using ink, chalk, or even markers.

## Foxy Thank You

Designer: Latisha Yoast

❶ Make card from cardstock. ❷ Trim cardstock and patterned paper strips; adhere. ❸ Stamp thank you. ❹ Tie ribbon around card; affix chipboard fox.

*Finished size: 3¾" x 4¾"*

## Yellow Hello

Designer: Lisa Dorsey

❶ Make card from cardstock. ❷ Trim patterned paper; adhere. Affix lace and adhere rhinestones. ❸ Emboss cardstock; die-cut butterfly and adhere to card. ❹ Ink alphabet; spell "Hello".
❺ Punch two flowers from cardstock; adhere together with foam tape and adhere to card. ❻ Cut cardstock strip, dampen with water, twist, and roll into flower; adhere. Adhere rose and pearls.

*Finished size: 6½" x 3¾"*

**SUPPLIES:** *Cardstock:* (Chiffon, Sunbeam) Bazzill Basics Paper *Patterned paper:* (Dreamland from Lullaby Lane collection) Webster's Pages *Clear stamp:* (thank you from Sophie's Sentiments set) Lawn Fawn *Dye ink:* (Tuxedo Black) Tsukineko *Sticker:* (chipboard fox) Cosmo Cricket *Fibers:* (yellow ribbon) Papertrey Ink

**SUPPLIES:** *Cardstock:* (Chiffon, Sunbeam, medium yellow) Bazzill Basics Paper *Patterned paper:* (Bright Golden Rays from 29th Street Market collection) My Mind's Eye *Chalk ink:* (yellow) Clearsnap *Accents:* (yellow roses) Prima; (clear rhinestones) Creative Charms; (white pearls) *Stickers:* (white lace) BasicGrey; (Daiquiri alphabet) American Crafts *Template:* (embossing swirl) Ellison *Die:* (butterfly) Ellison *Tool:* (flower punch) Marvy Uchida

DESIGNER TIP

Use just a corner of a sheet of decorative-edge paper as a card background. It adds a pretty touch and one sheet is enough for several cards.

## Celebrate Life

Designer: Betsy Veldman

❶ Make card from cardstock; cover with patterned paper. ❷ Trim patterned paper and adhere; zigzag-stitch edges. ❸ Stamp celebrate. Ink card edges. ❹ Trim patterned paper strip and adhere. Stamp flourish. ❺ Affix chipboard life; adhere pearls. ❻ Tie on ribbon. Thread button with twine and adhere.

*Finished size: 5½" x 4¼"*

## ⑤ Yellow Feel Better

Designer: Beth Opel

❶ Make card from patterned paper. ❷ Trim and adhere cardstock and patterned paper strips. ❸ Apply rub-on; adhere trims and ribbon. ❹ Attach brads, adhere flowers, and adhere rhinestones. ❺ Print sentiment on cardstock; punch into tag and adhere with foam tape. Knot ribbon and adhere.

*Finished size: 5" x 3½"*

**SUPPLIES:** *Cardstock:* (Vintage Cream) Bazzill Basics Paper *Patterned paper:* (Decorative Edge Cardstock from Fresh Print Clothesline collection) Little Yellow Bicycle; (Big Butterfly from Artsy Urban collection) GCD Studios; (Cabbage Rose from Paper Girl collection) The Girls' Paperie *Clear stamps:* (celebrate from Say It with Style set; flourish from Fancy Flourishes set) Papertrey Ink *Chalk ink:* (Creamy Brown) Clearsnap *Specialty ink:* (Dark Chocolate hybrid) Papertrey Ink *Accents:* (cream button) Papertrey Ink; (white pearls) Kaisercraft *Sticker:* (chipboard life) Little Yellow Bicycle *Fibers:* (cream twine, yellow ribbon) Papertrey Ink

**SUPPLIES:** *Cardstock:* (Chiffon, Lily White) Bazzill Basics Paper *Patterned paper:* (Solar from Sunny Days collection) GCD Studios; (Near Mint from The Thrift Shop collection) October Afternoon *Accents:* (yellow flower brads) Making Memories; (yellow velvet flowers) Maya Road; (clear rhinestones) Heidi Swapp *Rub-on:* (white leaf border) Hambly Screen Prints *Fibers:* (yellow polka dot ribbon) Offray; (yellow crochet trim) Fancy Pants Designs; (white crochet trim) Jo-Ann Stores; (yellow ribbon) Making Memories *Fonts:* (Miss Brooks) www.dafont.com; (CBX Memory) Chatterbox *Tool:* (tag punch) McGill

DESIGNER TIP

Using several different textures gives the card unexpected pizzazz.

## Soothing Sympathy

Designer: Teri Anderson

❶ Make card from cardstock. ❷ Trim cardstock panel, adhere cardstock, and round three corners. Adhere to card. ❸ Trim leaves from embossed cardstock; adhere. ❹ Stamp with sympathy on cardstock; adhere ribbon loop and adhere to card. ❺ Adhere pearls.

*Finished size: 5½" x 4¼"*

## Green Hi

Designer: Chan Vuong

❶ Make card from cardstock. ❷ Emboss cardstock; adhere. ❸ Trim patterned papers; adhere to card. ❹ Spell "Hi" with alphabet.

*Finished size: 5" square*

**SUPPLIES:** *Cardstock:* (Hillary, Limeade, Parakeet; Parakeet embossed) Bazzill Basics Paper; (white) Georgia-Pacific *Clear stamp:* (with sympathy from Kind Deed set) Clear & Simple Stamps *Dye ink:* (Old Olive) Stampin' Up! *Accent:* (green pearls) Queen & Co. *Fibers:* (green ribbon) Stampin' Up! *Tool:* (corner rounder punch) Marvy Uchida

**SUPPLIES:** *Cardstock:* (Parakeet) Bazzill Basics Paper; (light green) Core'dinations *Patterned paper:* (Measuring Up from Material Girl pad) Cosmo Cricket; (Green Large Polka Dot from Lush collection) My Mind's Eye *Accents:* (green corrugated alphabet) Jillibean Soup *Template:* (embossing polka dots) QuicKutz

PATTERN
Find the pattern for Kim Hughes's
Sweet Pear Card on p.192.

## Green to You

Designer: Teri Anderson

① Make card from cardstock. ② Trim patterned paper; adhere to
card. ③ Stamp sentiment circle, punch into circle, and mat with
punched cardstock circle; adhere. ④ Adhere ribbon and pearls.
⑤ Thread button with string and adhere.

*Finished size: 5½" x 4¼"*

## Sweet Pear

Designer: Kim Hughes

① Make card from patterned paper; trim corners to create
tag shape. ② Cut pear, following pattern. ③ Trim leaves from
cardstock; bend in center for added dimension. Adhere pear and
leaves. ④ Attach brad; spell "Sweets" with stickers.

*Finished size: 3¾" x 5½"*

**SUPPLIES:** *Cardstock:* (Hillary, Limeade, Parakeet) Bazzill Basics Paper; (white)
Georgia-Pacific *Patterned paper:* (Happy Christmas from Christmas Sleigh collection)
GCD Studios *Clear stamp:* (sentiment circle from Sentiments Small set) American Crafts
*Dye ink:* (Old Olive) Stampin' Up! *Accents:* (green pearls) Queen & Co.; (green button)
Buttons Galore & More *Fibers:* (green ribbon) Stampin' Up!; (green string) *Tool:* (circle
punches) Fiskars

**SUPPLIES:** *Cardstock:* (Parakeet) Bazzill Basics Paper *Patterned paper:*
(Petite Gingham Green) A Muse Artstamps; (Limeade Serenade) Doodlebug Design
*Accent:* (green fabric brad) GCD Studios *Stickers:* (Green at Heart alphabet)
BasicGrey

**DESIGNER TIP**
Funky embellishments and a graphic design create a look far from the sleepy, restful feeling typically associated with blue.

thank you

hello baby

## 🖐5️⃣ Blue Thank You
Designer: Beth Opel

❶ Make card from cardstock. ❷ Trim cardstock blocks; adhere with foam tape. ❸ Adhere frame. Punch square from cardstock and mat with cardstock; adhere. ❹ Attach brads to flower; adhere. ❺ Affix sticker sentiment.

*Finished size: 4" square*

## 🖐5️⃣ Hello Baby Blue
Designer: Kim Kesti

❶ Make card from cardstock. ❷ Trim patterned paper panel; mat with cardstock. ❸ Adhere acrylic star to cardstock, trim, and adhere to. ❹ Affix sticker to cardstock; adhere to panel. ❺ Tie twine around panel and adhere panel to card.

*Finished size: 4" x 5¾"*

**SUPPLIES:** *Cardstock:* (Arctic, Jacaranda, Starmist, Lily White) Bazzill Basics Paper *Accents:* (blue rubber frame, blue rubber flower) KI Memories; (white brads) American Crafts *Sticker:* (thank you) SRM Press *Tool:* (square punch) EK Success

**SUPPLIES:** *Cardstock:* (Starmist, Jacaranda) Bazzill Basics Paper *Patterned paper:* (Boy Geometric from Snugglebug Boy collection) Little Yellow Bicycle *Accent:* (acrylic star) Little Yellow Bicycle *Sticker:* (hello baby) Little Yellow Bicycle *Fibers:* (white/blue twine) Making Memories

DESIGNER TIPS

Consider what moods, feelings, and images colors conjure up when working with monochromatics. The water image and dream sentiment fit the soothing shades of blue used in this card.

For a more earthy feel, change the blues on this card to greens to mimic the look of grass.

## Blue Super Star

Designer: Kelley Eubanks

① Make card from cardstock. Round bottom corners and ink edges. ② Stamp mini star across card. ③ Stamp star on cardstock; punch into star and adhere with foam tape. ④ Stamp sentiment on cardstock; punch into rounded rectangle and adhere with foam tape.

*Finished size: 3½" square*

## Blue Dream

Designer: Stephanie Halinksi

① Make card from cardstock. ② Trim patterned paper; apply glitter to top. Adhere. ③ Thread button with floss; adhere. ④ Affix dream sticker.

*Finished size: 5½" x 4¼"*

**SUPPLIES:** *Cardstock:* (Arctic, Jacaranda, Starmist) Bazzill Basics Paper *Clear stamps:* (polka dot star, mini star, sentiment from Star Prints set) Papertrey Ink *Dye ink:* (Pacific Point) Stampin' Up! *Tools:* (corner rounder, rounded rectangle punches) Stampin' Up!; (star punch) Fiskars

**SUPPLIES:** *Cardstock:* (Starmist) Bazzill Basics Paper *Patterned paper:* (Tangerine Tidal Wave from Heat Wave collection) American Crafts *Accent:* (blue button) BasicGrey; (clear glitter) Martha Stewart Crafts *Sticker:* (chipboard dream) Me & My Big Ideas *Fibers:* (blue floss)

## Thanks From the Heart

Designer: Maile Belles

❶ Make card from cardstock; cover with cardstock. ❷ Stamp many thanks and sentiment. ❸ Die-cut flourishes from cardstock. Stamp flourishes, emboss, and adhere with foam tape. ❹ Adhere rhinestones to metal flowers; adhere to card.

*Finished size: 5½" x 4¼"*

## Groovy Girl

Designer: Teri Anderson

❶ Make card from cardstock. Adhere patterned paper and cardstock strips. ❷ Punch two circles from cardstock, trim, and adhere. ❸ Fringe cardstock strips, layer, and adhere. ❹ Affix peace sticker and spell sentiment with alphabet stickers. ❺ Tie on floss.

*Finished size: 4¼" x 5½"*

**SUPPLIES:** *Cardstock:* (Grape Slush) Bazzill Basics Paper; (Plum Pudding) Papertrey Ink; (white) *Clear stamps:* (flourishes, many thanks, sentiment from Embellishments set) Papertrey Ink *Dye ink:* (Dusty Concord) Ranger Industries *Watermark ink:* Tsukineko *Embossing powder:* (clear) Jo-Ann Stores *Accents:* (purple metal flowers) Making Memories; (purple rhinestones) Kaisercraft *Dies:* (flourishes) Papertrey Ink

**SUPPLIES:** *Cardstock:* (Velvet, Jubilee, Grape Slush, Grape Jelly embossed) Bazzill Basics Paper; (white) Georgia-Pacific *Patterned paper:* (Funky Buttons/Blue Skies from Free Spirit collection) Little Yellow Bicycle *Stickers:* (Free Spirit alphabet, peace sign) Little Yellow Bicycle *Fibers:* (purple floss) DMC *Tools:* (fringe scissors) Martha Stewart Crafts; (circle punch) Fiskars

**DESIGNER TIP**

Cut long, thin strips of patterned paper and adhere to your card with the strips hanging off the edge. Your ribbon will hide the slanted edges, and you can get an even cut by turning the card over.

## ⑤ Vintage Thank You
Designer: Susan R. Opel

❶ Make card from cardstock; print "Thank you". ❷ Trim and adhere patterned paper; adhere ribbon. ❸ Adhere felt flowers. Attach fabric brad through flower and adhere; adhere brads. ❹ Affix rhinestones.

*Finished size: 5½" x 4¼"*

## ⑤ Touch of Lavender
Designer: Vanessa Menhorn

❶ Make card from cardstock. Cut rectangle of cardstock, punch edge, and adhere. ❷ Mat panel of patterned paper with cardstock; adhere. ❸ Die-cut oval and scalloped oval from cardstock. Stamp lavender and sentiment on oval, mat with scalloped oval, and adhere. ❹ Adhere pearls.

*Finished size: 4¼" x 5½"*

**SUPPLIES:** *Cardstock:* (white) *Patterned paper:* (Butterfly Kisses from Pixie-Licious collection) Cosmo Cricket; (Countdown from Socialite collection) Bella Blvd *Accents:* (purple fabric flower, brad; antique copper brads) Little Yellow Bicycle; (purple felt flowers) American Crafts; (purple rhinestones) K&Company *Fibers:* (purple ribbon) QVC *Font:* (Signet Roundhand) www.fonts101.com

**SUPPLIES:** *Cardstock:* (Heidi, Velvet, Jubilee) Bazzill Basics Paper; (cream) *Patterned paper:* (purple medallions from Guide Lines collection) Papertrey Ink *Clear stamps:* (lavender from Life collection, congratulations from Delightful Dahlia collection) Papertrey Ink *Dye ink:* (Dusty Concord) Ranger Industries *Accents:* (purple pearls) Prima *Dies:* (oval, scalloped oval) Spellbinders *Tool:* (border punch) Fiskars

**DESIGNER TIP**
Crumple seam binding with your
hand before tying for a vintage look.

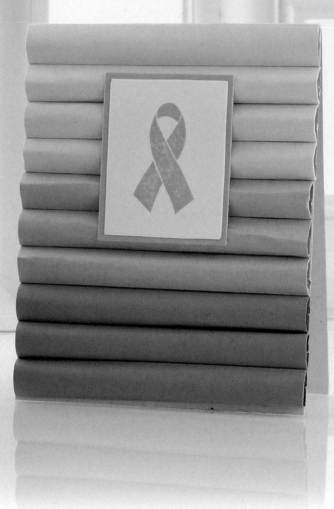

### 5 STEPS Thinking Pink

Designer: Julia Stainton

*Ink all paper edges.*
1 Make card from cardstock. 2 Cut cardstock rectangle, mat with cardstock, and stitch. Adhere. 3 Apply rub-on sentiment. 4 Tie seam binding bow; adhere. Adhere flowers and insert pins.

*Finished size: 5½" x 4¼"*

### 5 STEPS Full of Hope

Designer: Alison Anderson

1 Make card from cardstock. 2 Cut cardstock strips and score edges. Fold at score lines and wrap around awl to create bubble shape. Adhere scored edges to card. 3 Die-cut rectangle from cardstock; stamp Ribbon of Hope. Mat with die-cut cardstock rectangle and adhere to card.

*Finished size: 4¼" x 5½"*

**SUPPLIES:** *Cardstock:* (Pinkini, Fussy, Chablis) Bazzill Basics Paper *Dye ink:* (Brushed Corduroy) Ranger Industries *Accents:* (coral flowers) Prima; (clear crystal trinket pins) Maya Road *Rub-on:* (sentiment) Melissa Frances *Fibers:* (pink seam binding) Schiff Ribbons

**SUPPLIES:** *Cardstock:* (Pinkini, Fussy, Chablis, Lily White) Bazzill Basics Paper *Rubber stamp:* (Ribbon of Hope) Stampin' Up! *Pigment ink:* (Pretty in Pink) Stampin' Up! *Dies:* (rectangles) Spellbinders *Tool:* (awl)

**DESIGNER TIP**

Cut multiple flowers at once in order to save time and make them more consistent in size.

**DESIGNER TIP**

If you plan to allow elements of your design to hang off, cut the card a little narrow so that it will fit in a standard-size envelope.

## Too Kind

Designer: Windy L. Robinson

❶ Make card from cardstock. ❷ Cut cardstock square slightly smaller than card front. Make roses from cardstock, adhere to square. Adhere square to card. ❸ Stamp sentiment on cardstock and cut into tag. ❹ Tie on ribbon; adhere tag. ❺ Adhere button and rhinestone.

*Finished size: 5" square*

## A Friend Always

Designer: Julia Stainton

❶ Make card from cardstock. ❷ Cut cardstock rectangle, punch cardstock circle, and adhere. ❸ Sand edges of sticker, affix, and staple. ❹ Apply rub-on sentiment.

*Finished size: 3½" x 5½"*

**SUPPLIES:** *Cardstock* (Pinkini, Fussy, Chablis) Bazzill Basics Paper *Clear stamp:* (sentiment from Mega Mixed Messages set) Papertrey Ink *Pigment ink:* (Vintage Sepia) Tsukineko *Accents:* (clear button) The Girls' Paperie; (pink rhinestone) Michaels *Fibers:* (pink ribbon) Michaels

**SUPPLIES:** *Cardstock:* (Pinkini, Fussy, Chablis) Bazzill Basics Paper *Accents:* (silver staples) *Rub-on:* (sentiment) American Crafts *Sticker:* (pink chipboard scalloped circle) Lily Bee Design *Tool:* (2½" circle punch) Marvy Uchida

## Floral Thanks

Designer: Teri Anderson

1 Make card from cardstock; round one corner. 2 Die-cut and punch circles from cardstock; adhere. 3 Adhere tag. 4 Spell "Thanks" with stickers. *Note: Adhere cardstock behind letter 'a'.* 5 Adhere pearls.

*Finished size: 4¼" square*

## With Sympathy

Designer: Latisha Yoast

1 Make card from cardstock. 2 Cut rectangle of cardstock; emboss and adhere. 3 Adhere flower trim, stamp with sympathy, and adhere pearls.

*Finished size: 6" x 4"*

**SUPPLIES:** *Cardstock:* (Smoky, Cashmere, Brown) Bazzill Basics Paper *Accents:* (floral tag) Ormolu; (white pearls) Kaisercraft *Stickers:* (Jack & Jill alphabet) Doodlebug Design *Die:* (circle) QuicKutz *Tools:* (circle punch) Fiskars; (corner rounder punch) Marvy Uchida

**SUPPLIES:** *Cardstock:* (Smoky) Bazzill Basics Paper; (white) Gina K Designs *Clear stamp:* (with sympathy from Communique Curves Sentiments set) Papertrey Ink *Dye ink:* (Tuxedo Black) Tsukineko *Accents:* (brown pearls) BasicGrey *Fibers:* (brown flower trim) Webster's Pages *Template:* (embossing fleur-de-lis) Spellbinders

## ⑤ Thank You Flowers

Designer: Julia Stainton

❶ Make card from cardstock; ink edges. ❷ Apply rub-ons.
❸ Die-cut flower from corrugated cardstock; adhere. ❹ Tie twine
bow; adhere bow and flower. ❺ Spell "Thank you" with stickers.

*Finished size: 6" x 3½"*

## ⑤ Happy Birthday Dad

Designer: Tiffany Johnson

❶ Make card from cardstock; print "Happy birthday". ❷ Cut
rectangle of cardstock; emboss and adhere. ❸ Cut rectangle
of cardstock; stamp image, emboss, round corner, and punch
border. Adhere. ❹ Spell "Dad" with stickers.

*Finished size: 4¼" x 5½"*

**SUPPLIES:** *Cardstock:* (Stormy) Bazzill Basics Paper; (kraft corrugated) Creative Imaginations *Dye ink:* (Brushed Corduroy) Ranger Industries *Accent:* (white flower) Prima *Rub-ons:* (brown floral, zebra swatches) Hambly Screen Prints *Stickers:* (Bliss alphabet) American Crafts *Fibers:* (natural twine) Westrim Crafts *Die:* (flower) Provo Craft

**SUPPLIES:** *Cardstock:* (Stormy, Cashmere) Bazzill Basics Paper; (white) Clear & Simple Stamps *Clear stamp:* (dad and son from Hero Dad set) Clear & Simple Stamps *Specialty ink:* (Perfect Little Black Dress hybrid) Clear & Simple Stamps *Stickers:* (Clothesline alphabet) Little Yellow Bicycle *Font:* (Roxy) Creating Keepsakes *Templates:* (embossing diamond plate) Provo Craft; (embossing woodgrain) Papertrey Ink *Tools:* (border punch) Stampin' Up!; (corner rounder punch) EK Success

### ⁵⁵ₛₜₑₚₛ Cream Floral Wishes

Designer: Windy Robinson

❶ Make card from cardstock. ❷ Cut strips of cardstock; layer and adhere. ❸ Adhere pearls and flowers. ❹ Stamp sentiment.

*Finished size: 5½" x 4¼"*

### ⁵⁵ₛₜₑₚₛ Natural Friends

Designer: Maren Benedict

❶ Make card from cardstock. ❷ Cut curved piece of cardstock; stamp Grainy Background and adhere. ❸ Stamp banner and "Friends" on cardstock; cut out, thread pieces with twine, and adhere. Tie twine bows and adhere. ❹ Stamp foxes on card. Stamp foxes on cardstock; cut out and adhere pieces. ❺ Stamp clouds on cardstock; cut out and adhere. *Note: Adhere some clouds with foam tape.*

*Finished size: 4¼" x 5½"*

**SUPPLIES:** *Cardstock:* (Smoky, Twig, French Vanilla) Bazzill Basics Paper *Clear stamp:* (best wishes from Fillable Frames #4 set) Papertrey Ink  *Pigment ink:* (Vintage Sepia) Tsukineko  *Accents:* (white pearls) Mark Richards; (cream flowers) Prima

**SUPPLIES:** *Cardstock:* (Smoky, Twig, French Vanilla) Bazzill Basics Paper  *Rubber stamps:* (banner, letters from A Little Happy set; clouds, foxes from Togetherness Families set; Grainy Background) Unity Stamp Co.  *Dye ink:* (London Fog) Tsukineko  *Watermark ink:* Tsukineko  *Fibers:* (cream twine) Papertrey Ink

BONUS IDEA
Use a transparency for a fun twist on your favorite patterns.

BONUS IDEA
Use this simple design for a subtle party invitation, a thank-you card, or just because.

## Friends Forever

Designer: Tanis Giesbrecht

❶ Make card from cardstock. ❷ Cut square of cardstock; round top corners. ❸ Cut strip of cardstock; stamp Giving It All Meaning and emboss. Adhere to square. ❹ Punch circles from cardstock; adhere to square. ❺ Stitch border and adhere square to card. ❻ Die-cut butterfly from cardstock; stamp Grainy Background, emboss, and adhere. ❼ Stamp friends forever on cardstock; cut out and adhere.

*Finished size: 4¼" square*

## Polka Dot Thanks

Designer: Tiffany Johnson

❶ Make card from transparency sheet. ❷ Cut rectangle of cardstock; adhere inside card. ❸ Cut strip of cardstock; staple and adhere. ❹ Die-cut circle from cardstock; stamp circles and thank you. Adhere with foam tape.

*Finished size: 4¾" x 5½"*

**SUPPLIES:** *Cardstock:* (Smoky, Twig, French Vanilla) Bazzill Basics Paper *Rubber stamps:* (friends forever from Happily Ever After set, Giving It All Meaning, Grainy Background) Unity Stamp Co. *Dye ink:* (Basic Grey) Stampin' Up! *Watermark ink:* Tsukineko *Embossing powder:* (Seafoam White) Ranger Industries *Die:* (butterfly) Provo Craft *Tools:* (1" circle punch) EK Success; (corner rounder punch) Making Memories

**SUPPLIES:** *Cardstock:* (Smoky, Twig, French Vanilla) Bazzill Basics Paper *Transparency sheet:* (Antique White Mod Circles) Hambly Screen Prints *Clear stamps:* (circles from Vintage Circles Small set) Waltzingmouse Stamps; (thank, you from Generosity set) Clear & Simple Stamps *Dye ink:* (London Fog) Tsukineko *Accents:* (silver mini staples) Tim Holtz *Die:* (circle) Spellbinders

### With Sympathy
Designer: Lisa Johnson

1 Make card from cardstock. 2 Cut rectangle of cardstock; round bottom corners and score lines. 3 Stamp icons and with sympathy on piece, tie on ribbon, and adhere with foam tape.

*Finished size: 4¼" x 5½"*

### Thinking of You
Designer: Kelley Eubanks

1 Make card from cardstock. 2 Cut square of cardstock; round corners, stamp chain link, and adhere with foam tape. 3 Die-cut butterfly from cardstock; adhere. 4 Stamp sentiment; emboss. 5 Adhere rhinestones.

*Finished size: 4½" square*

**SUPPLIES:** *Cardstock:* (Harvest Gold, white) Papertrey Ink *Clear stamps:* (icons from Embellishments set, with sympathy from Mega Mixed Messages set) Papertrey Ink *Dye ink:* (gray) Marvy Uchida *Accent:* (amber rhinestone) Zva Creative *Fibers:* (brown ribbon) Creative Impressions *Tools:* (corner rounder punch) EK Success; (scorer) Scor-Pal Products

**SUPPLIES:** *Cardstock:* (Smoky, Sunflower, Chocolate Cream) Bazzill Basics Paper *Clear stamps:* (sentiment from Essential Messages set) Hero Arts; (chain link from Background Basics: Retro set) Papertrey Ink *Dye ink:* (Vintage Photo) Ranger Industries *Watermark ink:* Tsukineko *Embossing powder:* (white) Stewart Superior Corp. *Accents:* (clear rhinestones) Kaisercraft *Die:* (butterfly) Stampin' Up! *Tool:* (corner rounder punch) Stampin' Up!

DESIGNER TIP
Adhere only the body of the butterflies for a touch of dimension.

## Bee Happy

Designer: Betsy Veldman

❶ Make card from cardstock; ink edges. ❷ Cut rectangles of patterned paper; ink edges and adhere. Stamp bees. ❸ Adhere trim, rickrack, and ribbon. Wrap card with twine. ❹ Stamp bee and bee happy on journaling card. Mat journaling card with patterned paper; trim mat with decorative-edge scissors and adhere. ❺ Thread buttons with twine; adhere.

*Finished size: 4¼" x 5½"*

## Perfect

Designer: Maren Benedict

❶ Make card from cardstock. ❷ Cut strips of cardstock; punch borders and adhere. ❸ Stamp butterfly three times on cardstock; cut out and adhere. ❹ Stamp sentiment.

*Finished size: 4¼" x 5½"*

**SUPPLIES:** *Cardstock:* (Vintage Cream) Papertrey Ink *Patterned paper:* (Henna from Origins collection) BasicGrey; (Favorite Thing Colorful Umbrellas from Quite Contrary collection; French Flea Market from Bella Bella French Flea Market collection) My Mind's Eye *Clear stamps:* (bees, bee happy from Honey Bees set) Papertrey Ink *Chalk ink:* (Creamy Brown) Clearsnap *Specialty ink:* (Smokey Shadow, Summer Sunrise hybrid) Papertrey Ink *Accents:* (brown, yellow, white buttons) Papertrey Ink; (circle journaling card) *Fibers:* (gray rickrack, measuring tape ribbon) Little Yellow Bicycle; (cream crocheted trim) Fancy Pants Designs; (cream twine) Papertrey Ink *Tool:* (decorative-edge scissors) Provo Craft

**SUPPLIES:** *Cardstock:* (Smoky, Sunflower, Chocolate Cream, Lily White) Bazzill Basics Paper *Rubber stamps:* (butterfly, sentiment from Perfect Just the Way You Are set) Unity Stamp Co. *Dye ink:* (Tuxedo Black) Tsukineko *Pigment ink:* (white) Stampin' Up! *Tool:* (border punch) Martha Stewart Crafts

# Find Your Style

What goes into a certain style? Do ruffles make it cute? Does satin make it elegant? How, exactly, do you make something shabby chic? Take the quiz below and find out if your style leans toward fun and cute, clean and graphic, shabby chic and vintage, or classy and elegant.

**When you design your projects, you think in terms of:**
A. Simple and/or playful
B. Plenty of "white space"
C. Layers, layers, layers!
D. Sophisticated combinations

**The pattern that draws your eye most frequently is:**
A. Polka dots or gingham
B. Those that are bold and geometric
C. Soft and oversized floral
D. Damask

**Your sentiment text is usually:**
A. Full of doodles and whimsy
B. No-frills
C. Soft and scripty
D. Stately and formal

**Your favorite embellishments are:**
A. Buttons and hearts
B. Simple shapes and icons
C. Lace and found items
D. Glitter and bling

**When you use fibers on a project, they are:**
A. Pompom trim and rickrack
B. Bold ribbon and simple string
C. Jute twine and twill ribbon
D. Satin and velvet ribbon

**Count the number of As, Bs, Cs, and Ds you chose, and tally your score below.**

A _____      B _____

C _____      D _____

**Mostly A:** you and your happy color scheme are definitely fun & cute *(find out more on p.72)*
**Mostly B:** a little goes a long way with your clean & graphic designs *(find out more on p.92)*
**Mostly C:** your soft comfortable style is shabby chic or vintage *(find out more on p.130)*
**Mostly D:** your style pedigree is classy & elegant *(find out more on p.116)*

The sparkling embellishments, sophisticated font, and polished ribbon make this card amazingly **Classy and Elegant.**

The whimsical clouds, simple shapes, and friendly gingham make this card **Fun and Cute** to boot!

The distressed edges, antique lace trim, and retro image make this card super **Shabby and Vintage.**

The clean lines, simple text, and bold blocks of color make this one trendy **Clean and Graphic** card.

# Fun & Cute

What makes a fun and cute card? To begin with—a happy color scheme, a sweet sentiment, and an uncomplicated design. Throw in some whimsy (like cartoons and doodles), a few simple shapes (like hearts and stars), some friendly patterns (like polka dots and gingham)—and voila! There's a smile on your face and a song in your heart that's unmistakably fun and cute.

## DESIGNER TIP

When stitching by hand, pierce holes first with a paper piercer to ensure even stitches. It also prevents sore fingertips from pushing the needle through the paper, especially when it's going through several layers.

## 5 STEPS Birdie Hello

Designer: Teri Anderson

❶ Make card from cardstock. ❷ Wrap floss around card front to create lines. ❸ Punch circles from patterned paper; trim and adhere. ❹ Stamp hello. ❺ Affix sticker.

*Finished size: 4¼" square*

## 5 STEPS Chirp Up!

Designer: Tanis Giesbrecht

❶ Make card from cardstock. ❷ Cut square of patterned paper; stitch border with floss and adhere. ❸ Punch circle and scalloped circle from cardstock; layer and adhere. ❹ Apply hen rub-on; spell "Chirp up!" with rub-ons. ❺ Thread button with floss; fold ribbon and adhere

*Finished size: 4½" square*

**SUPPLIES:** *Cardstock:* (white) Bazzill Basics Paper *Patterned paper:* (Strawberry Jam, Ice Cream from Fly a Kite collection; Near Mint from Thrift Shop collection) October Afternoon *Clear stamp:* (hello from Essential Messages set) Hero Arts *Dye ink:* (Tuxedo Black) Tsukineko *Sticker:* (bird) American Crafts *Fibers:* (white floss) DMC *Tool:* (circle punch) Fiskars

**SUPPLIES:** *Cardstock:* (Leapfrog) Bazzill Basics Paper; (Very Vanilla) Stampin' Up! *Patterned paper:* (Farm House from Farm Fresh collection) October Afternoon *Accent:* (pink button) *Rub-ons:* (Purkey alphabet) American Crafts; (red hen) October Afternoon *Fibers:* (green floss, red ribbon) *Tools:* (1³⁄₈" circle punch, scalloped circle punch) Stampin' Up!

**DESIGNER TIP**

When you make felt embellishments, use a non-synthetic felt. It will give you a nice, clean edge.

## Birthday Banner

Designer: Julie Campbell

❶ Make card from cardstock. ❷ Cut cardstock panel; tie on twine. Trim felt strip and triangles; adhere. ❸ Adhere borders, using foam tape for one. Adhere panel to card. ❹ Stamp happy birthday on cardstock. Trim and adhere with foam tape. ❺ Die-cut scalloped circle from felt. Stitch edges with floss and adhere with foam tape. ❻ Affix face sticker and adhere party hat with foam tape.

*Finished size: 4¼" x 5½"*

**SUPPLIES:** *Cardstock:* (Grandma's Rocker) Core'dinations; (white) Papertrey Ink; (teal) *Rubber stamp:* (happy birthday from Tag! You're It! set) Cornish Heritage Farms *Chalk ink:* (Dark Brown) Clearsnap *Accents:* (red, orange scalloped borders) Bazzill Basics Paper *Stickers:* (chipboard face, party hat) Martha Stewart Crafts *Fibers:* (white floss) Scrapworks; (brown twine) *Die:* (scalloped circle) Spellbinders *Other:* (assorted felt) Heather Bailey

## Your Day to Shine

Designer: Kim Kesti

❶ Make card from cardstock; cover front with patterned paper. ❷ Cut strip of cardstock; punch border and adhere. ❸ Cut rectangle of cardstock; round top corners, apply shimmer spray, and adhere when dry. ❹ Stamp lanterns on cardstock; color with markers and apply dimensional glaze. Thread floss through lanterns; adhere lanterns with foam tape. ❺ Attach brads; affix sticker.

*Finished size: 4½" x 5½"*

**SUPPLIES:** *Cardstock:* (red, white) Bazzill Basics Paper *Patterned paper:* (multi stripe) *Rubber stamps:* (lanterns from Three Paper Lanterns set) Hero Arts *Solvent ink:* (Jet Black) Tsukineko *Specialty ink:* (Jazz Blue shimmer spray) Tattered Angels *Color medium:* (assorted markers) Copic *Accents:* (black brads) Doodlebug Design *Sticker:* (sentiment) SRM Press *Fibers:* (black floss) Karen Foster Design *Tools:* (embossing border punch) EK Success; (corner rounder punch) *Other:* (dimensional glaze) Ranger Industries

DESIGNER TIP

To achieve a soft torn edge, crease the paper first and then tear it.

## :5: Dude, You Rock!

Designer: Lisa Johnson

❶ Make card from cardstock. ❷ Ink edges of patterned paper panels and adhere. ❸ Punch circles from patterned paper and adhere with foam tape. ❹ Stamp sentiment on cardstock; punch right edge and adhere. ❺ Thread buttons with twine and adhere.

*Finished size: 4¼" x 5½"*

**SUPPLIES:** All supplies from Papertrey Ink unless otherwise noted. *Cardstock:* (Spring Rain, white) *Patterned paper:* (Bundle, Bots from Lil' Buddy collection) Pebbles Inc. *Clear stamp:* (sentiment from Signature Greetings set) *Pigment ink:* (Fresh Snow) *Specialty ink:* (Smokey Shadow hybrid) *Accents:* (orange buttons) *Fibers:* (white twine) *Tool:* (1½" circle punch) Marvy Uchida

## :5: Friends til the End

Designer: Courtney Kelley

❶ Make card from cardstock. ❷ Tear cardstock strip and adhere. Round right corners. ❸ Stamp sentiment. ❹ Stitch flower stems with floss. Tie on floss. ❺ Adhere flowers with foam tape. Adhere buttons.

*Finished size: 5" x 4¼"*

**SUPPLIES:** *Cardstock:* (Hillary, kraft) Bazzill Basics Paper *Rubber stamp:* (sentiment from Delightful Moments set) Unity Stamp Co. *Solvent ink:* (Timber Brown) Tsukineko *Accents:* (blue, pink flowers) Sassafras Lass; (yellow, orange buttons) *Fibers:* (brown floss) DMC *Tool:* (corner rounder punch) We R Memory Keepers

DESIGNER TIP
Bright, citrus colors complement each other nicely, offering a fun and feminine look.

## Cute Cupcake

Designer: Tiffany Johnson

❶ Make card from cardstock. ❷ Trim patterned paper panel to fit card. Tie on ribbon and trim ends with decorative-edge scissors. ❸ Stamp scallops on cardstock; mat with cardstock and adhere with foam tape. ❹ Affix cupcake. Tie button with twine and adhere. ❺ Adhere panel.

*Finished size: 4¼" square*

**SUPPLIES:** *Cardstock:* (Tulip) Close To My Heart; (white) *Patterned paper:* (Airhead from Sugar Rush collection) BasicGrey *Clear stamp:* (scallops from Boutique Borders set) Close To My Heart *Dye ink:* (Blush) Close To My Heart *Accent:* (pink button) BasicGrey *Sticker:* (felt cupcake) Sassafras Lass *Fibers:* (pink ribbon) Michaels; (pink floss) DMC *Tool:* (decorative-edge scissors) Fiskars

## Embrace Happiness

Designer: Rebecca Oehlers

❶ Make card from cardstock. ❷ Stamp polka dots on cardstock; stitch border. ❸ Adhere buttons. Adhere branch and bird with foam tape. ❹ Double-mat piece with cardstock and adhere with foam tape. ❺ Stamp embrace happiness on cardstock. Stitch edges and mat with cardstock. Adhere with foam tape.

*Finished size: 4¼" x 5½"*

**SUPPLIES:** All supplies from Papertrey Ink unless otherwise noted. *Cardstock:* (Dark Chocolate, Hibiscus Burst, Summer Sunrise, white) *Clear stamps:* (embrace happiness from Mega Mixed Messages set; polka dots from Polka Dot Basics II set) *Pigment ink:* (Hibiscus Burst) *Specialty ink:* (Summer Sunrise hybrid) *Accents:* (pink felt bird, brown felt branch) Sassafras Lass; (orange, pink buttons)

## Birthday Cupcake

Designer: Rebecca Oehlers

① Make card from cardstock; round left corners. ② Emboss cardstock panel; round left corners. Adhere patterned paper strips and zigzag-stitch seams. ③ Adhere ribbon and adhere panel with foam tape. ④ Emboss cardstock. Die-cut into label; adhere with foam tape. ⑤ Stamp happy birthday on cardstock. Trim and adhere with foam tape. ⑥ Die-cut label from cardstock. Stamp cupcake; color. Stamp cupcake on patterned paper, trim, and adhere. Thread button with twine and adhere. Adhere label with foam tape.

*Finished size: 7" x 5"*

## 5 STEPS You're Sweet

Designer: Wendy Sue Anderson

① Make card from cardstock. ② Cut patterned paper panel. Adhere patterned paper and cardstock strips; affix border sticker. Stitch edges. ③ Print repeating sentiment on photo paper; trim and adhere. Zigzag-stitch edge. ④ Tie on ribbon and affix ribbon sticker. Adhere panel.

*Finished size: 4¼" x 6¼"*

**SUPPLIES:** *Cardstock:* (Pure Poppy, Rustic Cream) Papertrey Ink  *Patterned paper:* (Cherry Pie, Farmers Market, Ribbon Sandwich from Early Bird collection) Cosmo Cricket  *Clear stamps:* (cupcake from Baby Button Bits set; happy birthday from Birthday Basics set) Papertrey Ink  *Specialty ink:* (Dark Chocolate, Pure Poppy hybrid) Papertrey Ink  *Color medium:* (green, gray, red markers) Copic  *Accent:* (red button) Papertrey Ink  *Fibers:* (aqua ribbon, white twine) Papertrey Ink  *Template:* (Swiss Dots embossing) Provo Craft  *Dies:* (labels) Spellbinders  *Tool:* (corner rounder punch)

**SUPPLIES:** *Cardstock:* (white) American Crafts; (teal) Die Cuts With a View  *Patterned paper:* (Strawberry Fields, Sunday Picnic from Garden Variety pad) Cosmo Cricket  *Specialty paper:* (photo)  *Stickers:* (teal chipboard ribbon) Cosmo Cricket; (yellow glitter border) Doodlebug Design  *Fibers:* (red gingham ribbon)  *Font:* (SNF Goody) www. scrapnfonts.com

**DESIGNER TIP**
Embellishing the bicycle with chipboard flowers is a simple way to punch up the cute factor.

thank you

## ✦5 Sweet 16
Designer: Latisha Yoast

❶ Make card from cardstock. ❷ Stamp banner on cardstock panel. Cut triangles from patterned paper and adhere. ❸ Spell "Sweet 16" with stickers. Affix banner sticker and tie on twill. ❹ Adhere panel with foam tape.

*Finished size: 3¾" x 6"*

**SUPPLIES:** *Cardstock:* (Sunflower embossed) Bazzill Basics Paper; (white) Flourishes *Patterned paper:* (Beehive Brunch from Dear Lizzy collection) American Crafts *Clear stamp:* (banner from Warble set) American Crafts *Dye ink:* (Broken China) Ranger Industries *Stickers:* (Regards alphabet, Chickadee alphabet, banner) American Crafts *Fibers:* (red twill) Papertrey Ink

## ✦5 Bicycle Thank You
Designer: Heidi Van Laar

❶ Make card from cardstock; cover with cardstock. ❷ Trim patterned paper and adhere. ❸ Trim wood papers. Stitch with crochet thread and adhere. ❹ Affix stickers. ❺ Stamp thank you on cardstock; trim into flag. Stitch flag to wood paper strip with crochet thread and adhere with foam tape.

*Finished size: 5½" square*

**SUPPLIES:** *Cardstock:* (red, yellow) American Crafts; (white) *Patterned paper:* (Creamy Coconut from Heat Wave collection) American Crafts *Specialty paper:* (Thin Birch, Thin Cherry wood from Real Wood collection) Creative Imaginations *Clear stamp:* (thank you from Everyday Sayings set) Hero Arts *Pigment ink:* (black) Clearsnap *Stickers:* (chipboard bicycle, flowers) American Crafts *Fibers:* (white crochet thread) Coats & Clark

## Forgetful Elephant

Designer: Julie Campbell

❶ Make card from cardstock ❷ Cut cardstock panel to fit card front; ink edges. Adhere cardstock strip. ❸ Punch edge of patterned paper strip and adhere. Stitch edges. ❹ Die-cut and emboss circle from cardstock. Stamp swirly circle and adhere. Spell sentiment with stickers. ❺ Die-cut and emboss circle from cardstock; ink edges and adhere with foam tape. ❻ Adhere thread around elephant sticker; affix. Trim hat from patterned paper and adhere with foam tape. ❼ Adhere pearls, tie on ribbon, and adhere panel.

*Finished size: 4¼" x 5½"*

**SUPPLIES:** *Cardstock:* (kraft) The Paper Company; (Rustic Cream) Papertrey Ink *Patterned paper:* (red polka dot from 2008 Bitty Dot Basics collection) Papertrey Ink *Clear stamp:* (swirly circle from Borders & Corners {circle} set) Papertrey Ink *Pigment ink:* (Fresh Snow) Papertrey Ink *Specialty ink:* (Pure Poppy hybrid) Papertrey Ink *Accents:* (white pearls) Kaisercraft *Stickers:* (felt elephant) Martha Stewart Crafts; (Tiny Type alphabet) Cosmo Cricket *Fibers:* (blue denim stitched ribbon) Cosmo Cricket *Dies:* (circles) Spellbinders *Tool:* (border punch) Fiskars

## Happy Anniversary

Designer: Julie Cameron

❶ Make card from cardstock; round bottom corners. ❷ Cut patterned paper to fit card front; adhere. ❸ Cut strip of cardstock; punch border and adhere. ❹ Cut rectangle of cardstock; print sentiment, stitch border, and adhere. ❺ Die-cut birds from cardstock; ink wings, adhere glitter, attach brads, and adhere with foam tape. ❻ Punch heart from cardstock; adhere glitter. Adhere with foam tape.

*Finished size: 4¼" square*

**SUPPLIES:** *Cardstock:* (Perfect Baby Boy Blue) Prism; (Teal, Bark, Crimson) Bazzill Basics Paper; (white) *Patterned paper:* (Sugar Sprinkles from Polar Expressions collection) Imaginisce *Pigment ink:* (Spring Rain) Papertrey Ink *Specialty ink:* (Reflection Blue hybrid) Stewart Superior Corp. *Accents:* (iridescent glitter) Duncan; (amber rhinestones) Crafts, Etc. *Font:* (Sunnydale) www.myfonts.com *Die:* (bird) QuickKutz *Tools:* (heart punch) Fiskars; (border punch) EK Success; (corner rounder punch) We R Memory Keepers

DESIGNER TIP
Mat your focal point with patterned paper to add some unexpected whimsy.

Mom, you are always in style!

.....follow your bliss

## Always in Style
Designer: Kelly Marie Alvarez

❶ Make card from cardstock; print sentiment. ❷ Die-cut label from patterned paper; adhere. ❸ Die-cut label from cardstock; stamp dress form and color with marker. Adhere with foam tape. ❹ Stamp dress form on scraps of patterned paper; cut out dress pieces and adhere.

*Finished size: 4¼" x 5½"*

## Follow Your Bliss
Designer: Tiffany Johnson

❶ Make card from cardstock; cover with patterned paper. ❷ Trim cloud from patterned paper and adhere. ❸ Apply rub-on and pierce holes.

*Finished size: 6" x 4½"*

**SUPPLIES:** *Cardstock:* (Sweet Blush) Papertrey Ink; (white) Neenah Paper *Patterned paper:* (Great Northern Beans from White Bean collection) Jillibean Soup; (Picking Pansies from Dear Lizzy collection) American Crafts *Clear stamp:* (dress form from Sew Lovely set) Lawn Fawn *Dye ink:* (black) *Color medium:* (peach marker) Copic *Font:* (Sweetheart Script) www.myfonts.com *Dies:* (labels) Spellbinders

**SUPPLIES:** *Cardstock:* (white) *Patterned paper:* (Growing Green from Dear Lizzy collection) American Crafts *Rub-on:* (sentiment) American Crafts

BONUS IDEA

For a more classic look, stamp the ghosts on white cardstock. These little guys are the perfect focal point for an invitation to a spooky party!

### 5 STEPS Trick or Treat
Designer: Kelly Marie Alvarez

❶ Make card from cardstock. ❷ Cut rectangle of cardstock; stamp ghosts. Draw arms to connect. ❸ Stamp ghosts on patterned paper; cut out and adhere to stamped piece with foam tape. ❹ Adhere stamped piece with foam tape. ❺ Spell sentiment with stickers.

*Finished size: 6½" x 3½"*

### 5 STEPS Bluebird Thanx
Designer: Courtney Kelley

❶ Make card from cardstock. ❷ Trim cardstock strips and adhere. Zigzag-stitch seam with floss. ❸ Cut clouds from patterned paper. Adhere and stitch with floss. ❹ Affix bird, hearts, and bubble. ❺ Spell "Thanx" with stickers.

*Finished size: 4¼" x 5¼"*

**SUPPLIES:** *Cardstock:* (Orange Zest) Papertrey Ink; (white) Neenah Paper *Patterned paper:* (Great Find, Still in Box, Needs Paint from Thrift Shop collection) October Afternoon; (Tiny Tulips, Cherry on Top from Homespun collection) Jenni Bowlin *Clear stamp:* (ghost from Stamp It: Halloween set) Hero Arts *Pigment ink:* (Pitch Black) Ranger Industries *Color medium:* (black pen) Sakura *Stickers:* (Piper chipboard alphabet) BasicGrey

**SUPPLIES:** *Cardstock:* (Artesian Pool, Lily Pad, brown) Bazzill Basics Paper *Patterned paper:* (Shower from Season collection) Crate Paper *Stickers:* (chipboard bluebird, cream conversation bubble, red heart, blue heart) Crate Paper; (Fabulous Mini alphabet) Chatterbox *Fibers:* (blue floss) DMC

## Gumball Thanks

Designer: Julie Campbell

❶ Make card from cardstock; round one corner. ❷ Print sentiment on patterned paper; trim and adhere. ❸ Die-cut rectangle from felt; trim and adhere. ❹ Trim strip from patterned paper and adhere. ❺ Die-cut and emboss circle from cardstock. Stamp gumball machine. Color and apply dimensional glaze. Adhere with foam tape. ❻ Adhere pearls.

*Finished size: 4½" square*

## Penguin Love

Designer: Laura O'Donnell

❶ Make card from cardstock. ❷ Cut rectangle of cardstock; stamp newsprint and adhere. ❸ Stamp penguins and hearts on cardstock; color with markers, cut out, and adhere with foam tape. ❹ Stamp penguins on scrap cardstock; cut out heart, color with marker, and adhere with foam tape.

*Finished size: 4" x 5½"*

**SUPPLIES:** *Cardstock:* (Aqua Mist, white) Papertrey Ink *Patterned paper:* (yellow polka dots from 2008 Bitty Dot Basics collection) Papertrey Ink; (Line Up from Monstrosity collection) Sassafras Lass *Clear stamp:* (gumball machine from Gumballs set) My Cute Stamps *Dye ink:* (Tuxedo Black) Tsukineko *Color medium:* (assorted markers) Copic *Accents:* (red pearls) Kaisercraft *Font:* (SNF Goody) www.scrapnfonts.com *Dies:* (scalloped rectangle, circle) Spellbinders *Tool:* (corner rounder punch) Other: (red felt) Heather Bailey; (dimensional glaze) Ranger Industries

**SUPPLIES:** *Cardstock:* (Basic Grey) Stampin' Up!; (white) *Rubber stamps:* (Penguin Love) Sugar Nellie; (hearts from The Birds and the Bees set; Newspaper Ads scrapblock) Cornish Heritage Farms *Dye ink:* (yellow) Stewart Superior Corp.; (Tuxedo Black) Tsukineko *Color medium:* (assorted markers) Copic

## Father's Day Hugs & Kisses

Designer: Alli Miles

❶ Make card from cardstock. ❷ Cut strips of cardstock; adhere. ❸ Stamp polka dots; attach brads. ❹ Die-cut and emboss label from cardstock; stamp typewriter, xoxo, and sentiment. Color with markers and adhere.

*Finished size: 4¼" x 5½"*

## Thanks Sew Much

Designer: Becky Olsen

❶ Make card from cardstock. ❷ Cut girl tag from patterned paper; adhere. ❸ Stitch flower stem with floss. ❹ Trim flower from patterned paper and adhere. Thread button with floss and adhere. ❺ Spell sentiment with stickers.

*Finished size: 4¼" x 5½"*

**SUPPLIES:** *Cardstock:* (Smokey Shadow, Ocean Tides, kraft, white) Papertrey Ink *Rubber stamp:* (typewriter from Simply Magical set) Unity Stamp Co. *Clear stamps:* (polka dots from Polka Dot Basics II set, xoxo from Sweet Love set, sentiment from Father Knows Best set) Papertrey Ink *Pigment ink:* (Fresh Snow) Papertrey Ink *Specialty ink:* (True Black hybrid) Papertrey Ink *Color medium:* (light gray, dark gray, pink markers) Copic *Accents:* (black brads) *Die:* (label) Spellbinders

**SUPPLIES:** *Cardstock:* (Vanilla) Cornish Heritage Farms *Patterned paper:* (Inspiration, Elements from Material Girl collection) Cosmo Cricket *Accents:* (blue button) Cosmo Cricket *Stickers:* (Tiny Type alphabet) Cosmo Cricket; (Darling alphabet) American Crafts *Fibers:* (pink floss) DMC

**DESIGNER TIP**

Creating a patchwork design is a great way to use your favorite patterned paper scraps.

## Baby Bunny

Designer: Julie Cameron

❶ Make card from cardstock; round bottom corners. ❷ Cut rectangle of cardstock; stamp stars, tie on ribbon, and adhere. ❸ Die-cut scalloped oval from cardstock; adhere glitter and adhere with foam tape. ❹ Die-cut bunny from cardstock; ink, color with markers and pen, and adhere glitter. Adhere with foam tape. ❺ Punch heart from cardstock; adhere glitter. Adhere to card. ❻ Stamp sentiment.

*Finished size: 4¼" square*

## Just a Note

Designer: Teri Anderson

❶ Make card from cardstock; adhere cardstock panel. ❷ Punch cardstock strips and adhere. ❸ Trim patterned paper pieces and adhere. ❹ Print sentiment on cardstock. Trim with decorative-edge scissors and adhere. ❺ Adhere rhinestones.

*Finished size: 3½" x 5½"*

**SUPPLIES:** *Cardstock:* (Perfect Baby Boy Light) Prism; (Fawn) Bazzill Basics Paper; (white) *Clear stamps:* (stars from Out on a Limb Additions set, sentiment from Baby Button Bits set) Papertrey Ink *Dye ink:* (Antique Linen) Ranger Industries *Pigment ink:* (Spring Rain) Papertrey Ink *Specialty ink:* (Burnt Umber hybrid) Stewart Superior Corp. *Color media:* (pink, black markers) Copic; (black felt-tip pen) Sanford *Accents:* (iridescent glitter) Duncan *Fibers:* (blue ribbon) Offray *Dies:* (scalloped oval) Spellbinders; (bunny) QuicKutz *Tools:* (heart punch) Fiskars; (corner rounder punch) We R Memory Keepers

**SUPPLIES:** *Cardstock:* (Vintage Cream) Papertrey Ink; (white) Georgia-Pacific *Patterned paper:* (Strawberry Jam, Sprinklers, Front Porch, Dandelions, Ice Cream from Fly a Kite collection) October Afternoon *Accents:* (blue rhinestones) Kaisercraft *Font:* (Oatmeal Cookie) www.twopeasinabucket.com *Tools:* (border punch) Martha Stewart Crafts; (decorative-edge scissors) Provo Craft

## :5: Season's Greetings Tree

Designer: Heidi Van Laar

① Make card from cardstock. ② Cut cardstock to fit card front, tie on ribbon, and adhere. ③ Stamp season's greetings on cardstock strip. Mat with cardstock, punch mat edges, and adhere with foam tape. ④ Die-cut circles from cardstock. Layer, trim into tree, and adhere with foam tape. ⑤ Thread button with twine and adhere.

*Finished size: 5" square*

**SUPPLIES:** *Cardstock:* (light green, dark green, teal, aqua) American Crafts; (white) Georgia-Pacific; (red) *Clear stamp:* (season's greetings from Holiday Sayings set) Hero Arts *Pigment ink:* (Cranberry) Clearsnap *Accent:* (yellow star button) Blumenthal Lansing *Fibers:* (white stitched ribbon) Michaels; (red/white twine) Martha Stewart Crafts *Dies:* (scalloped circles) Spellbinders *Tool:* (border punch) Fiskars

## Just Because

Designer: Lisa Johnson

① Make card from cardstock. Round top right corner and ink edges. ② Stamp background on cardstock; round top right corner and adhere. ③ Cut patterned paper panel and strip, ink edges, and adhere. Adhere rhinestones. ④ Punch circle from cardstock; ink edges. Adhere ribbon loop and adhere to card with foam tape. Thread button with twine and adhere. ⑤ Trim clouds from patterned paper, ink edges, and adhere. ⑥ Stamp just because on cardstock; trim and adhere. Adhere birds, using foam tape for one.

*Finished size: 4¼" x 5½"*

**SUPPLIES:** *Cardstock:* (Dark Chocolate, Ripe Avocado, kraft, white) Papertrey Ink *Patterned paper:* (clouds, stripes, floral from Treehouse collection) Pebbles Inc. *Clear stamps:* (just because from Asian Fusion set; diamond background from Background Basics: Tin Types set) Papertrey Ink *Dye ink:* (Creamy Caramel) Stampin' Up! *Specialty ink:* (Pure Poppy, Dark Chocolate hybrid) Papertrey Ink *Accents:* (blue, red birds) Pebbles Inc; (orange, green rhinestones) Zva Creative; (white button) Papertrey Ink *Fibers:* (red stitched ribbon, cream twine) Papertrey Ink *Tools:* (2½" circle punch, corner rounder punch) Marvy Uchida

DESIGNER TIP

Not only are swirly curly fonts cute, but they are also easy to overlap and link for a variety of looks.

## Deck the Halls

Designer: Gretchen Clark

❶ Make card from cardstock. ❷ Emboss cardstock; punch edge. Double-mat with cardstock. Tie on ribbon and adhere. ❸ Stamp ornaments and sentiment on cardstock; mat with cardstock and adhere with foam tape. ❹ Thread buttons with twine and adhere.

*Finished size: 4¼" x 5½"*

## Berry Sweet Friend

Designer: Wendy Sue Anderson

❶ Make card from cardstock. ❷ Adhere patterned paper strips; stitch edges. ❸ Trim and punch cardstock into tag; stitch. ❹ Spell sentiment on tag with stickers. Affix stickers; pierce holes, thread with twine, and tie. Attach brad. ❺ Apply glitter. Adhere tag with foam tape.

*Finished size: 6¼" x 4¼"*

**SUPPLIES:** *Cardstock:* (Hibiscus Burst, Aqua Mist, Dark Chocolate, white) Papertrey Ink; (Certainly Celery) Stampin' Up! *Clear stamps:* (ornaments, sentiment from Holiday Button Bits set) Papertrey Ink *Dye ink:* (Chocolate Chip) Stampin' Up! *Accents:* (green, pink, blue buttons) Papertrey Ink *Fibers:* (pink polka dot ribbon, hemp twine) Papertrey Ink *Template:* (Swiss Dots embossing) Provo Craft *Tool:* (border punch) Stampin' Up!

**SUPPLIES:** *Cardstock:* (white) American Crafts *Patterned paper:* (Cupcake Dot from Confections collection; Cherry Chocolate Dot, Cherry Pie Plaid from Cherries Jubilee collection) Doodlebug Design *Accents:* (strawberry epoxy brad) Doodlebug Design; (green glitter) Martha Stewart Crafts *Stickers:* (tags, swirl, flowers, Candy Shoppe alphabet) Doodlebug Design *Fibers:* (white twine) *Tool:* (border punch) Stampin' Up!

## One Big Hello

Designer: Rae Barthel

❶ Make card from cardstock; round bottom corners. ❷ Cut rectangle of patterned paper; round bottom corners and mat with patterned paper. Adhere. ❸ Cut strips of patterned paper and cardstock; punch borders and adhere. ❹ Tie on ribbon; adhere flower. ❺ Thread button with string; adhere. ❻ Spell "Hello" with stickers.

*Finished size: 4" x 6"*

**SUPPLIES:** *Cardstock:* (white) Bazzill Basics Paper *Patterned paper:* (Cherry Brownie, Cherry Tree, Cherry Sweet from My Sweet Cherry Pie collection) Nikki Sivils Scrapbooker *Accents:* (yellow daisy) Prima; (red button) Papertrey Ink *Stickers:* (June Bug alphabet) BasicGrey *Fibers:* (red gingham ribbon) Michaels; (white linen string) *Tools:* (border punch, corner rounder punch) EK Success

## Just Because Flowerpot

Designer: Windy L. Robinson

❶ Make card from cardstock; adhere patterned paper panel. ❷ Stamp just because and flowerpot on cardstock; ink edges. Double-mat with patterned paper and zigzag-stitch inner edge; adhere. ❸ Color heart and adhere button with foam tape. ❹ Tie on ribbon.

*Finished size: 5" square*

**SUPPLIES:** *Cardstock:* (kraft) DMD, Inc. *Patterned paper:* (Fireflies from Cottage collection) Crate Paper; (Petit Floral from Artsy Urban collection) GCD Studios; (Pattern Heart from Love Struck collection) Making Memories *Rubber stamp:* (flowerpot from Savor the Journey set) Unity Stamp Co. *Clear stamp:* (just because from Everyday Sayings set) Hero Arts *Dye ink:* (Walnut Stain) Ranger Industries *Chalk ink:* (Chestnut Roan) Clearsnap *Color medium:* (blue pen) Sakura *Accent:* (red flower button) Making Memories *Fibers:* (red polka dot ribbon) Offray

## Sweet Snowman

Designer: Kim Hughes

❶ Make card from patterned paper; cut ½" from bottom of card front. ❷ Cut tree and trunk from cardstock; adhere. ❸ Cut snowman from patterned paper and adhere. ❹ Adhere cardstock strip. Tie on ribbon. ❺ Adhere buttons.

*Finished size: 5" x 4¼"*

## Count Your Rainbows

Designer: Julie Campbell

❶ Make card from cardstock; cover with cardstock. ❷ Stamp sentiment and rainbow on cardstock panel. Color rainbow and apply glitter. ❸ Punch patterned paper and adhere to panel. Tie on ribbon and adhere panel to card.

*Finished size: 4½" x 5½"*

**SUPPLIES:** *Cardstock:* (Hazard scalloped, Sour Apple, Truffle) Bazzill Basics Paper *Patterned paper:* (Winter Wonderland from Let It Snow collection) Three Bugs in a Rug *Accents:* (red buttons) Papertrey Ink *Fibers:* (yellow striped ribbon) Strano Designs

**SUPPLIES:** *Cardstock:* (black, white) Papertrey Ink *Patterned paper:* (Over the Rainbow from Happy Place collection) Sassafras Lass *Rubber stamp:* (rainbow from Nothing but Blue Skies set) Unity Stamp Co. *Clear stamp:* (sentiment from Friendly Advice set) Inkadinkado *Dye ink:* (Tuxedo Black) Tsukineko *Specialty ink:* (Pure Poppy hybrid) Papertrey Ink *Color medium:* (assorted markers) Copic *Accent:* (clear glitter) Martha Stewart Crafts *Fibers:* (red ribbon) Papertrey Ink *Tool:* (embossing border punch) EK Success

**DESIGNER TIP**

Having a problem with stickers warping or not staying down on your card? Add a little adhesive to really anchor the edges.

## I Look Up To You

Designer: Angie Hagist

❶ Make card from cardstock. ❷ Cut rectangle of patterned paper; adhere. ❸ Cut giraffes from patterned paper; adhere. Note: Adhere neck of small giraffe with foam tape. ❹ Apply glitter glue and spell "Dad" with stickers. ❺ Cut strips of patterned paper; punch borders and adhere. ❻ Write sentiment on cardstock; trim, edge with pen, and adhere.

*Finished size: 5" x 5½"*

**SUPPLIES:** *Cardstock:* (Sunflowers Medium, Tawny Light) Prism *Patterned paper:* (giraffe, monkey from Zoo Pals pad) SEI *Color media:* (brown marker) Marvy Uchida; (gold pen) *Accent:* (gold glitter glue) Ranger Industries *Stickers:* (Shin-Dig alphabet) Doodlebug Design *Tool:* (border punch) EK Success

## ⑤ Bright & Cheery Get Well

Designer: Teri Anderson

❶ Make card from cardstock. ❷ Cut rectangles of patterned paper; adhere. ❸ Cut strip of patterned paper; adhere. ❹ Affix flower sticker; thread button with floss and adhere. ❺ Cut strip of cardstock; spell "Get well" with stickers, tie on ribbon, and adhere.

*Finished size: 5½" square*

**SUPPLIES:** *Cardstock:* (white) Georgia-Pacific; (Rustic Cream) Papertrey Ink *Patterned paper:* (Slow Motion from Enjoy Life collection) My Little Shoebox; (Moss from Green at Heart collection) BasicGrey; (yellow polka dot from Kitchen collection) A Muse Artstamps *Accent:* (green button) Buttons Galore & More *Stickers:* (flower, Green at Heart alphabet) BasicGrey *Fibers:* (green printed ribbon) American Crafts; (white floss) DMC

**DESIGNER TIP**
Punch small half-circle notches to wrap string around. That way, it won't slide.

## With Sympathy

Designer: Julie Cameron

❶ Make card from cardstock; round bottom corners. ❷ Cut strip of cardstock; punch border and adhere. ❸ Cut rectangle of patterned paper; adhere and stitch two edges. ❹ Die-cut label from cardstock; stamp tree and sentiment and adhere with foam tape. ❺ Punch flowers and butterfly from cardstock; adhere. ❻ Adhere rhinestones.

*Finished size: 4¼" square*

## An Apple a Day

Designer: Wendy Sue Anderson

❶ Make card from cardstock. ❷ Cut rectangles of patterned paper; adhere together. ❸ Punch border and half-circles; wrap string around and tie bow. Adhere to card. ❹ Trim and adhere journaling card; zigzag-stitch edge. Spell sentiment with stickers. ❺ Adhere apple charm.

*Finished size: 3¾" x 5½"*

**SUPPLIES:** *Cardstock:* (Spring Moss, Sweet Blush, kraft) Papertrey Ink; (Pinata) Bazzill Basics Paper; (white) *Patterned paper:* (Fauna from Zoofari collection) Doodlebug Design *Clear stamps:* (tree, with sympathy from Beyond Basic Borders set) Papertrey Ink *Specialty ink:* (Burnt Umber hybrid) Stewart Superior Corp.; (Ripe Avocado hybrid) Papertrey Ink *Accents:* (pink rhinestones) Crafts, Etc. *Die:* (label) Spellbinders *Tools:* (border punch) Martha Stewart Crafts; (butterfly punch) Carl Manufacturing; (flower punch) Fiskars; (corner rounder punch) We R Memory Keepers

**SUPPLIES:** *Cardstock:* (Chestnut) American Crafts *Patterned paper:* (apples, pink plaid from Greenhouse pad) K&Company *Accents:* (green apple charm, green border journaling card) October Afternoon *Stickers:* (Old West alphabet) Adornit-Carolee's Creations *Fibers:* (tan string) *Tools:* (border punch) Stampin' Up!; (⅛" circle punch)

## Way To Go

Designer: Julie Cameron

❶ Make card from cardstock. ❷ Cut strip of cardstock; punch border and adhere. ❸ Cut rectangle of patterned paper; adhere. ❹ Stamp stems and sentiment. ❺ Punch flowers from cardstock; adhere. ❻ Adhere rhinestones.

*Finished size: 4¼" square*

## Hello Baby

Designer: Lisa Johnson

❶ Make card from cardstock. ❷ Cut rectangle of cardstock; emboss background, tie on ribbon, and adhere with foam tape. ❸ Die-cut frame from cardstock; stamp frame, hello, and baby, and adhere with foam tape. ❹ Open project in software; drop in elephant, resize, and print on cardstock. Cut out, emboss, and adhere with foam tape. ❺ Cut ear shape from cardstock; adhere with foam tape. Adhere pearl. ❻ Thread button with twine; adhere.

*Finished size: 4¼" x 5½"*

**SUPPLIES:** *Cardstock:* (Dark Chocolate) Papertrey Ink; (yellow) Bazzill Basics Paper; (white) *Patterned paper:* (Humpty Dumpty from Baby collection) American Crafts *Clear stamps:* (flower stems from Blooming Button Bits set, sentiment from Star Prints set) Papertrey Ink *Pigment ink:* (Raspberry Fizz) Papertrey Ink *Specialty ink:* (Landscape hybrid) Stewart Superior Corp. *Accents:* (red rhinestones) *Tools:* (border punch) Fiskars; (flower punch) EK Success

**SUPPLIES:** All supplies from Papertrey Ink unless otherwise noted. *Cardstock:* (Lemon Tart, Spring Moss, white) *Clear stamps:* (hello, frame from Fillable Frames #1 set; baby from Mega Mixed Messages set) *Pigment ink:* (Fresh Snow, Spring Moss) *Accents:* (green button); (blue pearl) Zva Creative *Digital element:* (elephant from Rock-a-Bye Baby set) *Fibers:* (aqua ribbon, cream twine) *Software:* (scrapbooking) no source *Templates:* (Tin Types embossing); (Swiss Dots embossing) Provo Craft *Die:* (frame)

## ⁵⁵ Sparkly Jack

Designer: Maren Benedict

❶ Make card from cardstock. ❷ Cut rectangle and strips of patterned paper; adhere. *Note: Bend some bottom edges up slightly for dimension.* ❸ Color jack-o'-lantern with marker; apply glitter glue and adhere to card. ❹ Spell "Boo" with alphabet; color, draw dots, and adhere. ❺ Tie on ribbon.

*Finished size: 4¼" x 5½"*

**SUPPLIES:** *Cardstock:* (Smokey Shadow) Papertrey Ink *Patterned paper:* (Sesame from Kitchen Spice collection) BoBunny Press; (Escape from The Bat and the Weasels collection) Piggy Tales; (orange polka dot) *Color media:* (black, orange markers) Copic; (gold gel pen) *Accents:* (orange glitter glue) Ranger Industries; (chipboard jack-o'-lantern, Pop Art chipboard alphabet) Buzz & Bloom *Fibers:* (orange stitched ribbon) Papertrey Ink

## ⁵⁵ Pumpkin Boo

Designer: Alli Miles

❶ Make card from cardstock; round bottom corners. ❷ Stamp polka dots and sentiment. ❸ Cut strip of cardstock; punch border and adhere. ❹ Die-cut scalloped square from cardstock. Stamp pumpkin, color with markers, and adhere glitter. Adhere piece with foam tape. ❺ Adhere button and knotted ribbon.

*Finished size: 4¼" x 5½"*

**SUPPLIES:** *Cardstock:* (Orange Zest, black, white) Papertrey Ink *Rubber stamp:* (pumpkin from Autumn Trees set) Cornish Heritage Farms *Clear stamps:* (polka dots from Polka Dot Basics II set, boo! from Spooky Sweets set) Papertrey Ink *Pigment ink:* (Orange Zest) Papertrey Ink *Specialty ink:* (True Black hybrid) Papertrey Ink *Color medium:* (green, brown markers) Copic *Accents:* (rust button) Papertrey Ink; (orange glitter) Martha Stewart Crafts *Fibers:* (black polka dot ribbon) *Die:* (scalloped square) Spellbinders *Tools:* (border punch) Martha Stewart Crafts; (corner rounder punch) We R Memory Keepers

# Clean & Graphic

The clean and graphic style is characterized by the utilization of white space, clean lines, and simple treatment of text. It is no-frills, bare-boned, modern, and hip. And while you might be surprised at how minimally these cards are embellished, you might also be amazed at how quickly their messages are communicated.

### ⑤ Hello Little One
Designer: Jessica Witty

① Make card from cardstock. ② Stamp flower circles; emboss. ③ Stamp hello; emboss. ④ Color flower centers and hello with markers. ⑤ Stamp little one.

*Finished size: 3½" x 5"*

### ⑤ Mother's Day Birds
Designer: Jessica Witty

① Make card from cardstock. ② Trim cardstock, stamp sentiment, and adhere. ③ Punch birds from wood paper and adhere. ④ Punch birds from cardstock, trim one, and adhere.

*Finished size: 5" x 3½"*

**SUPPLIES:** *Cardstock:* (Soft Stone) Papertrey Ink *Clear stamps:* (circle flower, hello from Pop Flowers set) My Cute Stamps; (little one from Bitty Baby Blessings set) Papertrey Ink *Watermark ink:* Tsukineko *Embossing powder:* (white) Stampin' Up! *Color medium:* (Summer Sun, Pink Passion, Positively Pink, Pretty in Pink markers) Stampin' Up!

**SUPPLIES:** *Cardstock:* (Raspberry Fizz, kraft) Papertrey Ink *Specialty paper:* (Thin Birch wood from Real Wood collection) Creative Imaginations *Clear stamp:* (sentiment from Blooming Button Bits set) Papertrey Ink *Pigment ink:* (Raspberry Fizz) Papertrey Ink *Tool:* (birds punch) Martha Stewart Crafts

PATTERN

Find the pattern for Kim Kesti's
Brighten My Day Card on p.192

## 5 STEPS King of the Remote

Designer: Teri Anderson

❶ Make card from cardstock; adhere cardstock. ❷ Die-cut circle
from cardstock. ❸ Print sentiment on cardstock; adhere to circle
and trim. Mat piece with circle die-cut from cardstock; adhere to
card. ❹ Affix sticker.

*Finished size: 4¼" square*

## 5 STEPS Brighten My Day

Designer: Kim Kesti

❶ Make card from cardstock. ❷ Trim patterned paper slightly
smaller than front, mat with cardstock, and adhere. ❸ Cut light
bulb, following pattern; adhere with foam tape. ❹ Print sentiment
on cardstock, attach brads and adhere with foam tape.

*Finished size: 3¾" x 6¼"*

**SUPPLIES:** *Cardstock:* (white) Georgia-Pacific; (brown) Bazzill Basics Paper;
(teal, blue) WorldWin *Sticker:* (television) American Crafts *Font:* (Quirky) www.
twopeasinabucket.com *Dies:* (circles) QuicKutz

**SUPPLIES:** *Cardstock:* (Charcoal, Turquoise Mist, Silver Metallic, white)
Bazzill Basics Paper *Patterned paper:* (Odds & Ends from Home Front
collection) Studio Calico *Accents:* (silver brads) Making Memories *Font:*
(Aller) www.fontsquirrel.com

DESIGNER TIP
Combining letters and numbers in your sentiments is a great way to create an instantly graphic look.

## 5 STEPS Grin

Designer: Teri Anderson

❶ Make card from cardstock. ❷ Trim cardstock and round left corners; punch circle on edge and adhere piece. ❸ Attach brad. Affix camera and word bubble stickers. ❹ Spell sentiment with stickers.

*Finished size: 4¼" x 5½"*

## 5 STEPS Yay 4 You

Designer: Teri Anderson

❶ Make card from cardstock. ❷ Affix label sticker and spell sentiment with stickers. ❸ Trim patterned paper and adhere. Affix border sticker. ❹ Adhere ribbon and rhinestones.

*Finished size: 3¾" square*

**SUPPLIES:** *Cardstock:* (white) Georgia-Pacific; (red) WorldWin *Accent:* (black brad) Making Memories *Stickers:* (chipboard camera, word bubble) Cosmo Cricket; (black alphabet) Piggy Tales *Tools:* (corner rounder, ⅝" circle punches) Marvy Uchida

**SUPPLIES:** *Cardstock:* (white) Georgia-Pacific *Patterned paper:* (Compilation from Anthology collection) Studio Calico *Accents:* (red rhinestones) Kaisercraft *Stickers:* (gray number, grid label, gray stripe) Studio Calico; (Gumball alphabet) My Little Shoebox *Fibers:* (black ribbon) May Arts

DESIGNER TIP

Use the grid lines to line up embellishments and letters. This simple trick will make everything super straight and clean.

## 5 STEPS Get Well Mug

Designer: Courtney Kelley

❶ Make card from cardstock. Trim corners. ❷ Affix label sticker. ❸ Paint chipboard mug and adhere. ❹ Spell sentiment with stickers.

*Finished size: 4" square*

**SUPPLIES:** *Cardstock:* (kraft) Bazzill Basics Paper *Paint:* (Dash of Red) Ranger Industries *Accent:* (chipboard mug) Tim Holtz *Stickers:* (vintage label), (Tiny Circle alphabet) Jenni Bowlin Studio

## 5 STEPS Triple Birthday

Designer: Ryann Salamon

❶ Make card from cardstock. ❷ Trim rub-on and apply. ❸ Round top corners of cardstock panel. Stamp sentiment on panel; wrap with twine. Adhere to card with foam tape. ❹ Thread buttons with twine; adhere.

*Finished size: 5½" x 4¼"*

**SUPPLIES:** *Cardstock:* (white, kraft) Papertrey Ink *Rubber stamp:* (sentiment) Sugarloaf Products *Dye ink:* (Real Red) Stampin' Up!, (Rich Cocoa, Tuxedo Black) Tsukineko *Accents:* (red, brown buttons) Papertrey Ink; (black button) BasicGrey *Rub-on:* (texture grid) Hambly Screen Prints *Fibers:* (natural twine) Papertrey Ink *Tool:* (corner rounder punch) EK Success

### ⟨5 STEPS⟩ Birthdays Are Best

Designer: Dawn McVey

❶ Make card from cardstock. ❷ Stamp wood grain on cardstock panel; trim. ❸ Trim cardstock strip, punch edge, and adhere to panel. Adhere to card with foam tape. ❹ Stamp sentiment on cardstock. Trim, and adhere. ❺ Stamp Black and White Flowers on cardstock; trim and adhere with foam tape.

*Finished size: 4¼" square*

### ⟨5 STEPS⟩ Bright Stripe Thank You

Designer: Ryann Salamon

❶ Make card from cardstock. ❷ Wrap ribbon around card front; adhere. Tie on ribbon length. ❸ Spell sentiment with stickers. ❹ Adhere rhinestones.

*Finished size: 5½" x 4¼"*

**SUPPLIES:** *Cardstock:* (Hibiscus Burst, Vintage Cream, Rustic Cream, kraft) Papertrey Ink *Rubber stamps:* (wood grain from Artistic Windows set; Black and White Flowers) Hero Arts *Clear stamp:* (sentiment from Blooming Button Bits set) Papertrey Ink *Pigment ink:* (Hibiscus Burst) Papertrey Ink *Specialty ink:* (Dark Chocolate hybrid) Papertrey Ink *Tool:* (border punch) Fiskars

**SUPPLIES:** *Cardstock:* (white) Papertrey Ink *Accents:* (pink rhinestones) Kaisercraft *Stickers:* (Vera alphabet) American Crafts *Fibers:* (multi striped ribbon)

## Rainbow Get Well

Designer: Heidi Van Laar

① Make card from cardstock; cover with cardstock. ② Trim cardstock strips and adhere. ③ Trim cloud from patterned paper and adhere using foam tape. ④ Stamp sentiment. Adhere dots.

*Finished size: 4¼" x 5½"*

## Totally Awesome Birthday

Designer: Kim Kesti

① Make card from cardstock. ② Print sentiments on patterned paper, trim, and adhere. ③ Punch flowers from cardstock; attach with brads.

*Finished size: 6" square*

**SUPPLIES:** *Cardstock:* (red, orange, yellow, green, blue) American Crafts *Patterned paper:* (Creamy Coconut from Heat Wave collection) American Crafts *Clear stamp:* (sentiment from Everyday Sayings set) Hero Arts *Pigment ink:* (black) Clearsnap *Accents:* (clear acrylic dots)

**SUPPLIES:** *Cardstock:* (Tropical, Desert Marigold, Ladybug) Bazzill Basics Paper *Patterned paper:* (Hi from Everyday collection) American Crafts *Accents:* (pink, yellow brads) Making Memories *Font:* (Quicksand) www.fontspace.com *Tool:* (flower punch) EK Success

## ⑤ Simple Birthday Wishes

Designer: Alli Miles

❶ Make card from cardstock. ❷ Trim cardstock panel; stamp text. ❸ Stamp leaves and sentiment; adhere to card with foam tape.

*Finished size: 4¼" x 5½"*

## ⑤ Relax

Designer: Teri Anderson

❶ Make card from cardstock. ❷ Trim patterned paper to fit card front and adhere. ❸ Trim fabric sticker and affix. ❹ Punch circle from cardstock, cut in half , attach brads, and adhere. ❺ Spell "Relax" with stickers.

*Finished size: 2¾" x  6¼"*

**SUPPLIES:** All supplies from Papertrey Ink. *Cardstock:* (white) *Clear stamps:* (leaves from Turning a New Leaf set, sentiment from Vintage Picnic set, text from Background Basics: Text Style II set) *Dye ink:* (Chamomile) *Specialty ink:* (True Black, New Leaf hybrid)

**SUPPLIES:** *Cardstock:* (white) Georgia-Pacific *Patterned paper:* (Odds & Ends, Fab Strips from Home Front collection) Studio Calico *Accents:* (copper brads) Oriental Trading Co. *Stickers:* (striped fabric) Studio Calico; (Puff alphabet) SEI *Tool:* (circle punch) Martha Stewart Crafts

## Sleek Just Because

Designer: Rebecca Oehlers

❶ Make card from cardstock. ❷ Stamp leaves on cardstock piece. Trim image with craft knife. Stamp script. ❸ Stamp sentiment on cardstock; trim into flag. ❹ Adhere piece and flag to cardstock panel. Mat with cardstock and adhere to card with foam tape.

*Finished size: 4¼" x 5½"*

## Birthday Dots

Designer: Ashley C. Newell

❶ Make card from cardstock. ❷ Adhere cardstock strip. ❸ Trim cardstock panel and round right corners. Stamp beaded lines and sentiment. ❹ Tie on twill and adhere to card with foam tape.

*Finished size: 4¼" x 5½"*

**SUPPLIES:** *Cardstock:* (Spring Moss, True Black) Papertrey Ink *Clear stamps:* (leaves from Turning a New Leaf set, script from Background Basics: Text Style set, sentiment from Damask Designs set) Papertrey Ink *Watermark ink:* Tsukineko *Specialty ink:* (New Canvas hybrid) Stewart Superior Corp

**SUPPLIES:** *Cardstock:* (Berry Sorbet, Spring Moss, kraft) Papertrey Ink *Clear stamps:* (beaded lines from Background Basics: Retro set, sentiment from Communique Curves Sentiments set) Papertrey Ink *Pigment ink:* (black) Stampin' Up!; (red) *Fibers:* (black twill) Papertrey Ink *Tool:* (corner rounder punch) We R Memory Keepers

**DESIGNER TIP**

Create hand-stamped patterned paper by repeatedly stamping images from within a stamp set.

## Owl Thanks

Designer: Maile Belles

❶ Make card from cardstock. ❷ Stamp square and square outline repeatedly on card. ❸ Cut cardstock panel; round right corners. Stamp owl, circles, line, and sentiment. ❹ Stamp owl on cardstock, trim, and adhere to panel with foam tape. ❺ Adhere rhinestone and adhere panel to card with foam tape.

*Finished size: 4¼" x 5½"*

## Flower Burst Thank You

Designer: Lisa Johnson

❶ Make card from cardstock; round one corner. ❷ Mask strip across card front, stamp images, and remove mask. ❸ Score edges of masked area; apply glitter. ❹ Stamp sentiment. Adhere rhinestones.

*Finished size: 5½" x 4¼"*

**SUPPLIES:** *Cardstock:* (True Black, white) Papertrey Ink *Clear stamps:* (owl, circles, line, sentiment, square, square outline from Funky Flowers set) Wplus9 Design Studio *Pigment ink:* (Raspberry Fizz) Papertrey Ink *Watermark ink:* Tsukineko *Specialty ink:* (Summer Sunrise, True Black hybrid) Papertrey Ink *Accent:* (black rhinestone) Kaisercraft *Tool:* (corner rounder punch)

**SUPPLIES:** *Cardstock:* (white) Papertrey Ink *Clear stamps:* (sentiment from Asian Fusion set; assorted dot circles from Dot Spot set) Papertrey Ink *Pigment ink:* (Orange Zest, Raspberry Fizz, Plum Pudding) Papertrey Ink *Specialty ink:* (True Black hybrid) Papertrey Ink *Accents:* (purple, pink, orange rhinestones) Zva Creative; (silver glitter) Stewart Superior Corp. *Tools:* (corner rounder punch) Marvy Uchida; (scorer) Scor-Pal Products

**DESIGNER TIP**

Repeating the same element in different colors is a great way to create a graphic project.

## Butterfly Just Because

Designer: Layle Koncar

❶ Make card from cardstock; draw border. ❷ Punch butterflies from cardstock; adhere to card. ❸ Spell sentiment with stickers.

*Finished size: 4" square*

## Grateful for You

Designer: Jessica Witty

❶ Make card from cardstock. ❷ Trim strips of patterned paper, felt, and glitter cardstock. ❸ Stamp text on cardstock; trim into strip. Emboss cardstock, trim into strip. ❹ Adhere all strips. ❺ Stamp sentiment.

*Finished size: 5" x 3½"*

**SUPPLIES:** *Cardstock:* (pink, teal, burgundy, yellow, green, orange, red, aqua shimmer, peach) Bazzill Basics Paper *Stickers:* (Basics Micro Monogram alphabet) BasicGrey *Color medium:* (black pen) EK Success *Tool:* (butterfly punch) Martha Stewart Crafts

**SUPPLIES:** *Cardstock:* (white) Papertrey Ink; (Old Olive) Stampin' Up!; (silver glitter) Best Creation *Patterned paper:* (Lemon Meringue Pie from Nook & Pantry collection) BasicGrey *Clear stamps:* (sentiment from Friends 'Til the End set; text from Background Basics: Text Style II set) Papertrey Ink *Dye ink:* (Going Gray) Stampin' Up! *Template:* (Swiss Dots embossing) Provo Craft *Other:* (pink felt) Kunin Felt

PATTERN

Find the pattern for Beth Opel's
Thanks a Ton Card on p.192

## Thanks a Ton

Designer: Beth Opel

❶ Make card from cardstock. ❷ Trim patterned paper strip and adhere; trim cardstock rectangle and adhere. ❸ Make ton, following pattern; assemble. ❹ Spell "A ton" on ton with stickers, tie on ribbon, and adhere with foam tape. ❺ Trim cardstock strip; spell "Thanks" with stickers and adhere with foam tape. ❻ Affix epoxy dots.

*Finished size: 4½" x 5¾"*

## Heart Thank You

Designer: Angie Hagist

❶ Make card from cardstock. ❷ Print sentiment on cardstock; trim and adhere to card. ❸ Punch circle from cardstock, mat with punched cardstock circle, and adhere. ❹ Cover heart with cardstock; coat with dimensional glaze. Adhere to card.

*Finished size: 3½" x 8¼"*

**SUPPLIES:** *Cardstock:* (black) American Crafts; (aqua, kraft, brown, white) Bazzill Basics Paper *Patterned paper:* (Doorman from Metropolitan collection) American Crafts *Stickers:* (Patchwork alphabet) American Crafts; (Headline alphabet) Karen Foster Design; (black epoxy dots) Cloud 9 Design *Fibers:* (green ribbon) Making Memories

**SUPPLIES:** *Cardstock:* (white) American Crafts; (Dragonfly) Bazzill Basics Paper *Font:* (Tahoma) www.fonts.com *Accent:* (chipboard heart) Pebbles Inc. *Other:* (dimensional glaze) *Tools:* (circle punches) EK Success

**DESIGNER TIP**

Gently adhere punched circles behind the large circle, allowing you to re-adjust them to get the spacing just right before you adhere them permanently.

## Pink Circles Thank You

Designer: Layle Koncar

❶ Make card from cardstock. ❷ Trim patterned paper; adhere. ❸ Trim transparency sheet; adhere. ❹ Spell "Thank you." with stickers.

*Finished size: 6" square*

## Simple Just Because

Designer: Dawn McVey

❶ Make card from cardstock. ❷ Trim circle from cardstock; stamp sentiment. ❸ Punch circles from cardstock and adhere behind stamped circle to form flower. ❹ Adhere ribbon to card; notch ends. Adhere two loops of ribbon. ❺ Adhere flower with foam tape. Adhere buttons. ❻ Punch butterfly from cardstock; adhere.

*Finished size: 4¼" x 5½"*

**SUPPLIES:** *Cardstock:* (black) Bazzill Basics Paper *Patterned paper:* (Manifest from Basics collection) BasicGrey *Transparency sheet:* (Pink Chic Circles) Hambly Screen Prints *Stickers:* (Basics Mini Monogram alphabet) BasicGrey

**SUPPLIES:** All supplies from Papertrey Ink unless otherwise noted. *Cardstock:* (Summer Sunrise, Raspberry Fizz, Vintage Cream) *Clear stamp:* (sentiment from Mega Mixed Messages set) *Specialty ink:* (Dark Chocolate hybrid) *Accents:* (brown buttons) *Fibers:* (pink ribbon) *Tool:* (1" circle punch) Stampin' Up!; (butterfly punch) Martha Stewart Crafts

DESIGNER TIPS

When designing with a horizontal sentiment and striped paper, place the patterned paper so that the stripes are vertical to add contrast.

Ink a stamp with markers so that you can easily incorporate various colors.

## You Make Me Happy

Designer: Stephanie Halinski

❶ Make card from cardstock; round bottom corners. ❷ Trim patterned paper; adhere. ❸ Stamp sentiment on cardstock, using markers. Punch into oval and adhere with foam tape. ❹ Adhere rhinestone.

*Finished size: 4¼" x 5½"*

## Baby Circles

Designer: Charlene Austin

❶ Make card from cardstock. ❷ Punch circles from cardstock and adhere to cardstock panel; tie twill around panel and adhere. ❸ Spell "Baby" with stickers.

*Finished size: 4½" x 6"*

**SUPPLIES:** *Cardstock:* (Basic Gray, Whisper White) Stampin' Up! *Patterned paper:* (Sweater Weather from Jolly by Golly collection) Cosmo Cricket *Clear stamp:* (sentiment from Thanks Small set) American Crafts *Color medium:* (assorted markers) Stampin' Up! *Accent:* (clear rhinestone) *Tools:* (corner rounder, oval punches) Stampin' Up!

**SUPPLIES:** *Cardstock:* (Lemon Tart, Soft Stone, white) Papertrey Ink; (Basic Gray) Stampin' Up! *Stickers:* (multi-colored alphabet) Target *Fibers:* (yellow twill) Papertrey Ink *Tool:* (1½" circle punch) EK Success

DESIGNER TIP

The addition of an unexpected color to a traditional combination can take a simple design to the next level.

## 5 STEPS Let It Snow

Designer: Jessica Witty

❶ Make card from cardstock. ❷ Stamp polka dots; emboss. ❸ Cut cardstock strip, adhere twill, and adhere to card. ❹ Affix badges.

*Finished size: 5" x 3½"*

## 5 STEPS Woodgrain Thanks

Designer: Teri Anderson

❶ Make card from cardstock. ❷ Trim patterned paper, round right corners, and adhere. ❸ Score patterned paper strip along stripes. Fold and adhere. ❹ Affix man sticker. ❺ Spell sentiment with stickers.

*Finished size: 8½" x 3"*

**SUPPLIES:** *Cardstock:* (white) Papertrey Ink *Clear stamps:* (polka dots from Polka Dot Basics II set) Papertrey Ink *Watermark ink:* Tsukineko *Embossing powder:* (clear) Stampin' Up! *Stickers:* (tree, sentiment, yellow polka dot badges) American Crafts *Fibers:* (yellow twill) Papertrey Ink

**SUPPLIES:** *Cardstock:* (white) Georgia-Pacific *Patterned paper:* (Study Hall, Tube Socks from The Boyfriend collection) Cosmo Cricket *Stickers:* (chipboard man) Cosmo Cricket; (wood grain alphabet) Studio Calico *Tool:* (corner rounder punch) Marvy Uchida

## 5 STEPS Just Married

Designer: Angie Hagist

❶ Make card from cardstock. ❷ Trim cardstock, mat with cardstock and adhere. ❸ Affix heart and sentiment stickers.

*Finished size: 4¼" square*

## 5 STEPS Graduation Silhouette

Designer: Courtney Kelley

❶ Make card from cardstock; print sentiment. ❷ Die-cut graduate and hat from cardstock; adhere to card. ❸ Trim cardstock strip; adhere. Attach brads.

*Finished size: 4¼" x 5"*

**SUPPLIES:** *Cardstock:* (white) American Crafts; (Raven) Bazzill Basics Paper; (Clark metallic) Couture Cardstock *Stickers:* (red heart) October Afternoon; (just married) The Paper Studio

**SUPPLIES:** *Cardstock:* (white, gray shimmer) Die Cuts With a View *Accents:* (yellow brads) Queen & Co. *Dies:* (graduate, hat) Silhouette America

**DESIGNER TIP**

Combining rounded corners with
straight lines is a great way to create
a graphic look with basic supplies.

### Celebrate Kwanzaa

Designer: Teri Anderson

① Make card from cardstock. ② Cut cardstock block. Adhere
cardstock strips and rhinestones; adhere to card. ③ Adhere
cardstock strips. ④ Spell sentiment with stickers.

*Finished size: 5½" x 3¼"*

### Leafy Thinking of You

Designer: Alli Miles

① Make card from cardstock. ② Score four lines on card front.
Adhere cardstock strip. ③ Trim cardstock square; round corners.
Stamp leaf; emboss. Mat with cardstock, round mat corners, and
adhere. ⑤ Stamp sentiment.

*Finished size: 4¼" x 5½"*

**SUPPLIES:** *Cardstock:* (green) Bazzill Basics Paper; (white, black, red) WorldWin
*Accents:* (yellow rhinestones) *Stickers:* (Just My Type alphabet) Doodlebug Design

**SUPPLIES:** *Cardstock:* (white, black) Papertrey Ink *Clear stamps:* (leaf from Take
Three: Spring set, sentiment from Beyond Basics Borders set) Papertrey Ink *Watermark
ink:* Tsukineko *Specialty ink:* (True Black hybrid) Papertrey Ink *Embossing powder:*
(Lettuce) Ranger Industries *Tools:* (corner rounder punch) We R Memory Keepers;
(scorer) Scor-Pal Products

## 5 STEPS Feel Better Flower

Designer: Courtney Kelley

❶ Print sentiment on card. ❷ Trim patterned paper strip and adhere. ❸ Attach washer and brad to flower; adhere. ❹ Adhere wire.

*Finished size: 5½" x 4¼"*

## 5 STEPS Circles of Joy

Designer: Angie Hagist

❶ Make card from cardstock. ❷ Punch circles from cardstock; adhere to card. ❸ Die-cut "Joy" from cardstock; adhere.

*Finished size: 4½" x 3¾"*

**SUPPLIES:** *Patterned paper:* (Crazy Quilt from June Bug collection) BasicGrey *Accents:* (green paper flower) Sassafras Lass; (brass brad, washer) Tim Holtz *Font:* (Rockwell) www.fonts.com *Other:* (white card) Creative Café; (copper wire) Darice

**SUPPLIES:** *Cardstock:* (white) American Crafts; (Grass Green, Kisses) Bazzill Basics Paper *Dies:* (Chicken Noodle SkinniMini alphabet) QuicKutz *Tool:* (circle punch) EK Success

**DESIGNER TIP**

Think of alternate uses for specialty tools. The bows on these gifts were created with the punches designed for a bradmaker.

## Peaceful Snowflake

Designer: Heidi Van Laar

① Make card from cardstock; cover with cardstock. ② Trim cardstock panel. Stamp snowflake; emboss. Pierce snowflake trail; adhere panel to card. ③ Spell "Peace" with stickers.

*Finished size: 3¼" x 6"*

**SUPPLIES:** *Cardstock:* (Bazzill Red) Bazzill Basic Papers; (white) Georgia-Pacific *Clear stamps:* (snowflake from Merry & Bright set) We R Memory Keepers *Pigment ink:* (Cranberry) Clearsnap *Embossing powder:* (red) Jo-Ann Stores *Stickers:* (Metro Mini Shimmer alphabet) Making Memories

## Holiday Gifts

Designer: Beth Opel

① Make card from cardstock. ② Punch squares of various sizes from patterned papers; arrange and adhere. Trim card front along top edge of gifts. ③ Punch notched circles from cardstock; trim and adhere. ④ Adhere cardstock inside card.

*Finished size: 5" square*

**SUPPLIES:** *Cardstock:* (Luscious Lime Light, Medium) WorldWin; (red) American Crafts; (white) Bazzill Basics Paper *Patterned paper:* (No Pain, No Gain from Sports Edition collection) Teresa Collins Designs; (Bushels of Fun from Christmas collection; Cucumber Sandwiches from Spring & Summer collection; Red Rover from Kids collection) American Crafts; (Cold Water from White Bean collection) Jillibean Soup *Tools:* (square punches) EK Success; (notched circle punches) Imaginisce

DESIGNER TIP

Primary colors lend themselves well to clean and graphic projects.

## 5 STEPS Rainbow Friends

Designer: Angie Hagist

❶ Make card from cardstock. ❷ Trim cardstock strips and adhere. ❸ Spell "Friends" with stickers

*Finished size: 3¾" x 6"*

## 5 STEPS Bold Congrats

Designer: Kim Kesti

❶ Make card from cardstock; round bottom corners. ❷ Trim cardstock, round bottom corners, and adhere. Trim cardstock strip and adhere. ❸ Die-cut "Congrats" from cardstock; adhere cardstock behind some letters, and adhere.

*Finished size: 7" x 4"*

**SUPPLIES:** *Cardstock:* (white) American Crafts; (Rose Dark, Intense Kiwi, Carrot Cake, Mediterranean, Jelly, Lemon Drop) Bazzill Basics Paper *Stickers:* (Mini Market alphabet) October Afternoon

**SUPPLIES:** *Cardstock:* (Beetle Black, red, blue, yellow, white) Bazzill Basics Paper *Dies:* (Garden Mini alphabet) QuicKutz *Tool:* (corner rounder punch) We R Memory Keepers

DESIGNER TIP

DESIGNER TIP
This card can easily be customized for any graduate by using his/her school's colors.

DESIGNER TIP
To create a sentiment with brads, lightly sketch the letters you want to spell in pencil. After punching holes for brads, erase pencil lines and attach brads.

## Green Squares Congrats
Designer: Heidi Van Laar

❶ Make card from cardstock. ❷ Trim cardstock slightly smaller than front; adhere. ❸ Punch squares from cardstock. ❹ Spell "Congratulations" on squares with stickers. Adhere squares with foam tape.

*Finished size: 5" x 7"*

## Simple Joy
Designer: Kim Kesti

❶ Make card from cardstock. ❷ Trim cardstock pieces and adhere. ❸ Attach brads to spell "joy".

*Finished size: 6" x 3¾"*

**SUPPLIES:** *Cardstock:* (green) American Crafts; (white) Georgia-Pacific; (black) The Paper Company *Stickers:* (Casual alphabet) EK Success *Tool:* (¾" square punch)

**SUPPLIES:** *Cardstock:* (Kiwi, Cupcake, kraft, white) Bazzill Basics Paper *Accents:* (pink, green, white brads) Doodlebug Design

DESIGNER TIP

To achieve this graphic look, trim cardstock pieces in varying sizes of squares and rectangles. Arrange your pattern on the card and trim off excess from select pieces before adhering.

## ⑤ Mr. & Mrs.
Designer: Tiffany Johnson

❶ Make card from cardstock. ❷ Trim patterned paper to fit card front. ❸ Print sentiment on cardstock, trim and mat with cardstock; adhere.

*Finished size: 4¼" x 5½"*

## ⑤ Great Friend
Designer: Heidi Van Laar

❶ Make card from cardstock; cover with cardstock. ❷ Trim cardstock pieces, round opposite corners and adhere using foam tape. ❸ Stamp sentiment.

*Finished size: 4¼" x 5½"*

**SUPPLIES:** *Cardstock:* (light gray, dark gray) PaperTemptress; (white) Clear & Simple Stamps *Patterned paper:* (Muscari from I Do collection) American Crafts *Font:* (Century Gothic) www.fonts.com

**SUPPLIES:** *Cardstock:* (Nor'easter, Dragonfly, Sunbeam) Bazzill Basics Paper; (white) Georgia-Pacific *Clear stamp:* (sentiment from Thoughtful Messages set) Hero Arts *Chalk ink:* (Charcoal) Clearsnap *Tool:* (corner rounder punch) We R Memory Keepers

## Santa Joy

Designer: Angie Tieman

1 Make card from cardstock. 2 Tie ribbon around front.
3 Adhere calendar with foam tape. Attach clip. 4 Create
"Joy" label using label maker; affix.

*Finished size: 5¼" square*

## Love Memory

Designer: Kim Kesti

1 Make card from cardstock. 2 Trim patterned paper to fit card
front; adhere. 3 Print sentiment on cardstock; trim and adhere
using foam tape. 4 Die-cut bird from cardstock; adhere.

*Finished size: 4½" x 5¾"*

**SUPPLIES:** *Cardstock:* (Wild Wasabi) Stampin' Up! *Accents:* (santa calendar) Little
Yellow Bicycle; (white clip) Making Memories *Sticker:* (black label tape) DYMO
*Fibers:* (black/white striped ribbon) May Arts *Tool:* (label maker) DYMO

**SUPPLIES:** *Cardstock:* (French Vanilla scalloped, Beetle Black) Bazzill Basics Paper;
(white) *Patterned paper:* (Front Porch from Bayberry Cottage collection) Pink Paislee
*Die:* (bird) Making Memories *Font:* (Corbel) www.fonts.com

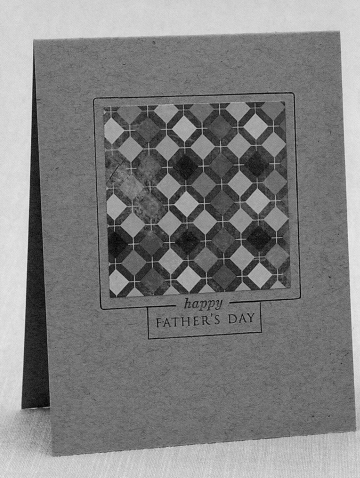

### Father's Day
Designer: Kimberly Crawford

① Make card from cardstock. ② Die-cut square from patterned paper and adhere. ③ Stamp sentiment. ④ Draw border with marker.

*Finished size: 4¼" x 5½"*

### Boom Box Greetings
Designer: Courtney Kelley

① Make card from cardstock. ② Trim patterned paper pieces and adhere. ③ Stamp sentiment. ④ Attach brads. ⑤ Draw frame around center piece.

*Finished size: 4¼" x 4¾"*

**SUPPLIES:** *Cardstock:* (kraft) Papertrey Ink *Patterned paper:* (Hopscotch from Friends Forever collection) Michaels *Clear stamp:* (sentiment from Father Knows Best set) Papertrey Ink *Specialty ink:* (Dark Chocolate hybrid) Papertrey Ink *Color medium:* (brown marker) *Die:* (large square) Spellbinders

**SUPPLIES:** *Cardstock:* (Pomegranate) Bazzill Basics Paper *Patterned paper:* (Elements, Homework, Borders from The Boyfriend collection) Cosmo Cricket *Rubber stamp:* (sentiment from Delightful Moments set) Unity Stamp Co. *Dye ink:* (Tuxedo Black) Tsukineko *Color medium:* (black pen) American Crafts *Accents:* (orange, green brads) Queen & Co.

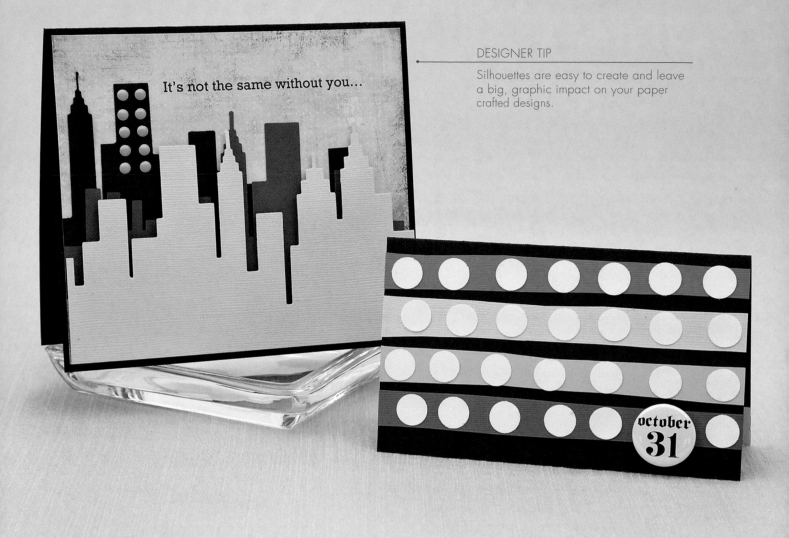

DESIGNER TIP

Silhouettes are easy to create and leave a big, graphic impact on your paper crafted designs.

It's not the same without you...

october 31

## ⁵ Without You

Designer: Kim Kesti

❶ Make card from cardstock. ❷ Print sentiment on patterned paper. Trim slightly smaller than card front; adhere. ❸ Die-cut skyline from two colors of cardstock; adhere. Die-cut skyline from cardstock and adhere using foam tape. ❹ Attach brads.

*Finished size: 6¼" x 5½"*

## ⁵ Striped Halloween

Designer: Kim Kesti

❶ Make card from cardstock. ❷ Trim cardstock strips and adhere. ❸ Punch circles from cardstock and adhere. ❹ Affix badge.

*Finished size: 5¾" x 3½"*

**SUPPLIES:** *Cardstock:* (Beetle Black, Vintage, Elephant) Bazzill Basics Paper *Patterned paper:* (Census from Basics collection) BasicGrey *Accents:* (yellow brads) *Font:* (Rockwell) www.fonts.com *Die:* (city skyline) QuicKutz

**SUPPLIES:** *Cardstock:* (Beetle Black, Festive, Mexican Poppy, Snapdragon, Vintage, white) Bazzill Basics Paper *Sticker:* (date badge) American Crafts *Tool:* (½" circle punch) Stampin' Up!

# Classy & Elegant

Classy & Elegant is a style that is polished. A shiny finish, sparkling embellishments, a rich color scheme, and sophisticated sentiment treatments are all part of the classy and elegant pedigree. Its look is regal, stunning, and dashing. And while its lines are clean, sweeping, and dramatic, it can also incorporate monochromatic color schemes with layered textures that awe and impress equally as well.

**DESIGNER TIP**

A sewing store or the button aisle at your local craft store is a great place to find unique and inexpensive buttons

## 5 STEPS · Pink & Green Joy

Designer: Windy Robinson

1. Cut card from cardstock and adhere patterned papers.
2. Spell "Joy" with stickers on acrylic page; adhere to card.
3. Tie on ribbon; thread buttons with floss and tie on.
4. Adhere rhinestones.

*Finished size: 5½" x 4¼"*

## 5 STEPS · Welcome, Precious Girl

Designer: Nina Brackett

1. Make card from cardstock. 2. Print sentiment on cardstock; cut into panel and punch bottom edge. 3. Cut patterned paper strip and adhere to panel. Adhere lace and tie on ribbon. 4. Adhere pearls and adhere panel to card.

*Finished size: 5½" x 4¼"*

**SUPPLIES:** *Cardstock:* (String of Pearls shimmer) Bazzill Basics Paper *Patterned paper:* (Evergreen from Eskimo Kisses collection) Basic Grey; (pink woodgrain from Handmade Cara Marie pad) K&Company *Accents:* (silver buttons) Blumenthal Lansing; (acrylic album page) Clear Scraps; (clear rhinestones) Mark Richards *Stickers:* (Glitter alphabet) Pink Paislee *Fibers:* (hot pink ribbon) Hobby Lobby; (gray floss) DMC

**SUPPLIES:** *Cardstock:* (Innocent Pink, Green Apple) Gina K Designs *Patterned paper:* (Tan Floral with Black Flocking from La Crème collection) Die Cuts With a View *Accents:* (white pearls) Mark Richards *Digital element:* (sentiment from Welcome Baby Sentiments kit) www.squigglefly.com *Fibers:* (cream lace, olive ribbon) *Tool:* (border punch) Fiskars

DESIGNER TIP

Change the sentiment and this design could easily be an elegant wedding, anniversary, or baby girl card.

DESIGNER TIP

Neutral card bases in colors like kraft or gray allow the richer colors of your paper and accents to take center stage.

## Pearly Birthday Wishes

Designer: Sarah Martina Parker

❶ Make card from cardstock. Emboss bottom and round bottom corners. ❷ Stamp roses on card to create background. ❸ Trim patterned paper panel, punch border, and adhere cardstock strip. ❹ Stamp birthday wishes on cardstock strip, adhere pearls, and adhere to panel. Adhere panel using foam tape. ❺ Tie on layered ribbons and adhere flower.

*Finished size: 4¼" x 5½"*

**SUPPLIES:** *Cardstock:* (Sweet Blush, white) Papertrey Ink *Patterned paper:* (Betty from Botanique collection) American Crafts *Clear stamps:* (birthday wishes from Giga Guide Lines set) Papertrey Ink; (rose from Summer Sentiments set) Clear & Simple Stamps *Pigment ink:* (Pixie Dust) Tsukineko *Accents:* (white pearls) Michaels; (cream flower) May Arts *Fibers:* (pink stitched ribbon) Papertrey Ink; (cream ribbon) *Template:* (Swiss Dots embossing) Provo Craft *Tools:* (border punch) Martha Stewart Crafts; (corner rounder punch) We R Memory Keepers

## Mom Valentine

Designer: Beth Opel

❶ Make card from cardstock; trim and adhere patterned paper. ❷ Trim die cut paper and adhere glitter cardstock behind; adhere to card. ❸ Adhere ribbon and pearls. ❹ Print sentiment on cardstock and mat with cardstock; adhere with foam tape.

*Finished size: 7" x 4"*

**SUPPLIES:** *Cardstock:* (kraft, cream, white) Bazzill Basics Paper; (pink glitter) Doodlebug Design *Patterned paper:* (Pink Swirl from Valentina collection) Anna Griffin *Specialty paper:* (Ivory Lace die cut from Valentina collection) Anna Griffin *Accents:* (white pearls) Hero Arts *Fibers:* (pink ribbon) American Crafts *Fonts:* (Engravers MT) www.myfonts.com; (Mutlu Ornamental) www.dafont.com

## Golden Anniversary

Designer: Jessica Witty

**1** Make card from cardstock; repeatedly stamp medallion and emboss. **2** Adhere glitter. **3** Stitch ribbon to card. **4** Stamp sentiment and insert pins.

*Finished size: 4" x 7"*

## Peacock Feather

Designer: Windy Robinson

**1** Make card from cardstock. **2** Trim patterned paper, ink edges, and adhere. **3** Adhere patterned paper strip, zigzag-stitch, and adhere pearls. **4** Tie on ribbon and adhere feather. **5** Thread buttons with twine, tie bow, and adhere with foam tape.

*Finished size: 3¾" x 7¼"*

**SUPPLIES:** *Cardstock:* (Naturals Ivory) Stampin' Up! *Clear stamps:* (medallion from Giga Guide Lines set, sentiment from Damask Designs set) Papertrey Ink *Watermark ink:* Tsukineko *Specialty ink:* (Dark Chocolate hybrid) Papertrey Ink *Embossing powder:* (clear) Stampin' Up! *Accents:* (gold glitter) Martha Stewart Crafts; (clear acrylic stick pins) Maya Road *Fibers:* (gold ribbon) Martha Stewart Crafts

**SUPPLIES:** *Cardstock:* (kraft) DMD, Inc. *Patterned paper:* (yellow damask, cream swirls from Handmade: Lofty Nest pad) K&Company *Chalk ink:* (Chestnut Roan) Clearsnap *Accents:* (peacock feather) K&Company; (copper button) Making Memories; (cream button) Blumenthal Lansing; (white pearls) Mark Richards *Fibers:* (white ribbon) Wrights; (twine) May Arts

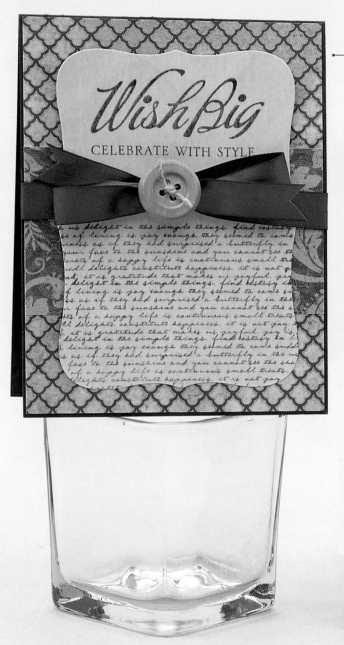

**DESIGNER TIP**

To stop the ink from bleeding on the wood paper, use a pigment or hybrid ink.

**DESIGNER TIP**

Make sure to use a heavy-duty corner rounding tool when rounding the corners of wood paper.

## Celebrate with Style

Designer: Kimberly Crawford

❶ Make card from cardstock. ❷ Adhere patterned paper strip to patterned paper panel. ❸ Stamp wish big, sentiment, and script on wood paper. Die-cut into label and adhere to panel. ❹ Tie ribbon on panel, thread button with twine, and tie to ribbon. ❺ Adhere panel.

*Finished size: 4¼" x 5½"*

**SUPPLIES:** *Cardstock:* (Enchanted Evening) Papertrey Ink *Patterned paper:* (Tudor Rose, Romantique from Renaissance Faire collection) Graphic 45 *Specialty paper:* (Thin Birch wood from Real Wood collection) Creative Imaginations *Clear stamps:* (wish big, sentiment from Big & Bold Wishes set; script from Background Basics: Text Style set) Papertrey Ink *Specialty ink:* (Enchanted Evening hybrid) Papertrey Ink *Accent:* (wood button) Blumenthal Lansing *Fibers:* (dark blue ribbon) Papertrey Ink; (twine) May Arts *Die:* (label) Spellbinders

## Floral & Woodgrain Wedding

Designer: Heidi Van Laar

❶ Make card from cardstock; cover with wood paper. ❷ Stamp sentiment. ❸ Punch flowers from cardstock, adhere, and adhere pearls. ❹ Round bottom corners.

*Finished size: 3½" x 6"*

**SUPPLIES:** *Cardstock:* (white) Georgia-Pacific *Specialty paper:* (Thin Birch wood from Real Wood collection) Creative Imaginations *Clear stamp:* (Mr. & Mrs. from Best Wishes set) Hero Arts *Pigment ink:* (Frost White) Clearsnap *Accents:* (white pearls) Kaisercraft *Tools:* (corner rounder punch) We R Memory Keepers; (hydrangea punch) Martha Stewart Crafts

**DESIGNER TIP**

Let a clever sentiment in a specialty font set the mood for your card. This Halloween greeting uses no witches, pumpkins, or black cats, yet the wording and font selection, paired with color choices, work together to complete a sophisticated seasonal design.

### Utterly Bewitching
Designer: Beth Opel

❶ Make card from cardstock. ❷ Trim and adhere patterned paper. ❸ Print sentiment on cardstock; mat with cardstock, using foam tape. Adhere to card with foam tape. ❹ Adhere trim and epoxy dots. ❺ Tie on ribbon.

*Finished size: 4¼" x 7"*

**SUPPLIES:** *Cardstock:* (black) American Crafts; (white) Bazzill Basics Paper; (orange) WorldWin *Patterned paper:* (Shake It Up from Tangerine Twist collection) Sandylion *Accents:* (black epoxy dots) Cloud 9 Design *Fibers:* (black ribbon) Offray; (orange scalloped trim) *Fonts:* (Chisel Wide Normal) www.letterpressfonts.com; (Modern No. 20) www.myfonts.com; (AL Fantasy Type) www.fonts101.com

### Filigree Birthday
Designer: Windy Robinson

❶ Make card from cardstock; adhere patterned paper. ❷ Trim patterned paper and adhere. Adhere loop trim and pearls. ❸ Stamp happy birthday on tag and adhere. ❹ Tie on ribbon. Thread button with floss and adhere.

*Finished size: 4¼" x 5½"*

**SUPPLIES:** *Cardstock:* (String of Pearls shimmer) Bazzill Basics Paper *Patterned paper:* (Love Potion from Cupid collection) Pink Paislee; (Jelly Beans from Sugar Rush collection) BasicGrey *Clear stamp:* (happy birthday from Sentiments 1 set) Stampavie *Specialty ink:* (Burnt Umber hybrid) Stewart Superior Corp. *Accents:* (white flower button) Making Memories; (gold border tag) Martha Stewart Crafts; (white pearls) Mark Richards *Fibers:* (orange ribbon) Hobby Lobby; (cream loop trim) Wrights; (cream floss)

## Pink Flower Happy Birthday

Designer: Sarah Martina Parker

❶ Make card from cardstock; adhere patterned paper. ❷ Adhere strip of patterned paper, adhere pearls across top, and apply glitter. ❸ Stamp happy birthday on cardstock, adhere pearls, and adhere using foam tape. ❹ Tie on ribbon. Adhere pearl flourishes. ❺ Layer flowers, attach brad, and adhere.

*Finished size: 4¼" x 5½"*

## Just a Note

Designer: Maren Benedict

❶ Make card from cardstock; cover with patterned paper.
❷ Adhere patterned paper piece and strip. ❸ Tie on ribbon.
❹ Stamp sentiment on patterned paper, trim, and adhere using foam tape.

*Finished size: 4¼" x 5½"*

**SUPPLIES:** *Cardstock:* (white) Papertrey Ink *Patterned paper:* (Linda's Homage from Juliette collection) SEI; (Roses from I Do collection) American Crafts *Clear stamp:* (happy birthday from Fancy Wishes set) Clear & Simple Stamps *Specialty ink:* (Smokey Shadow hybrid) Papertrey Ink *Accents:* (white pearl flourish, white flower, pink flower) Prima; (white pearls) Michaels; (white glitter) Doodlebug Design; (pink pearl brad) American Crafts *Fibers:* (brown ribbon) American Crafts

**SUPPLIES:** *Cardstock:* (Sweet Blush) Papertrey Ink *Patterned paper:* (Reflections, Established & True from Life's Portrait collection) Webster's Pages *Rubber stamp:* (sentiment from Noteworthy Occasion set) Unity Stamp Co. *Dye ink:* (Black Soot) Ranger Industries *Fibers:* (pink ribbon) May Arts

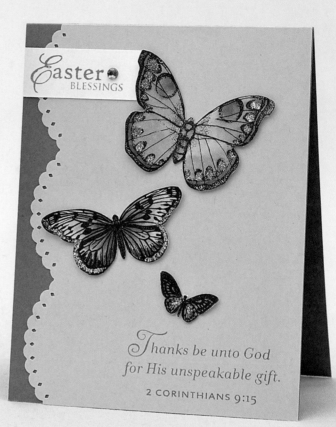

### Plum Birthday

Designer: Vanessa Menhorn

❶ Make card from cardstock; round bottom corners. ❷ Stamp background on cardstock; emboss. Round bottom corners and adhere patterned paper strip. ❸ Die-cut oval from cardstock; stamp sentiment. Mat with scalloped oval die-cut from cardstock and adhere using foam tape. ❹ Adhere pearls. ❺ Tie on ribbon and adhere panel.

*Finished size: 4¼" x 5½"*

**SUPPLIES:** *Cardstock:* (Plum Pudding, white, black) Papertrey Ink *Patterned paper:* (black polka dots from 2008 Bitty Dot Basics collection) Papertrey Ink *Rubber stamp:* (Antique Flower Background) Hero Arts *Clear stamp:* (sentiment from Bird Watching set) Papertrey Ink *Pigment ink:* (Graphite Black) Tsukineko *Watermark ink:* Tsukineko *Embossing powder:* (clear) Hero Arts *Accents:* (white pearls) Prima *Fibers:* (purple ribbon) Papertrey Ink *Dies:* (small oval, scalloped oval) Spellbinders *Tool:* (corner rounder punch)

### Easter Blessings

Designer: Dawn McVey

❶ Make card from cardstock. ❷ Cut cardstock panel, punch border, stamp sentiment, and adhere. ❸ Stamp Easter blessings on cardstock, trim, and adhere. Adhere rhinestone. ❹ Stamp butterflies on cardstock and color. Cut out, accent with glitter, and adhere.

*Finished size: 4¼" x 5½"*

**SUPPLIES:** *Cardstock:* (Spring Moss, Ripe Avocado, Vintage Cream) Papertrey Ink *Clear stamps:* (butterflies from Antique Engravings set) Hero Arts; (Easter blessings from Tags for Spring set; sentiment from Silent Night set) Papertrey Ink *Pigment ink:* (Plum Pudding) Papertrey Ink *Specialty ink:* (Ripe Avocado hybrid) Papertrey Ink *Color medium:* (assorted markers) Copic *Accents:* (purple rhinestone) Kaisercraft; (iridescent glitter) Papertrey Ink *Tool:* (border punch) EK Success

DESIGNER TIP

Sometimes making a classy card is easier than you would think—just find a double-sided patterned paper that you like and keep it simple by using the backside as its coordinating piece.

## Dramatic Love You

Designer: Windy Robinson

❶ Make card from cardstock; cover with patterned paper. ❷ Adhere patterned paper strip, round bottom corners, and adhere rhinestones. ❸ Tie on ribbon. ❹ Stamp love you on cardstock, trim, and ink edges. Adhere rhinestones and attach to button. ❺ Adhere button.

*Finished size: 4¼" x 5½"*

**SUPPLIES:** *Cardstock:* (kraft) DMD, Inc. *Patterned paper:* (Authentic from Origins collection) BasicGrey *Clear stamp:* (love you from Call Me set) Renaissance by Design *Dye ink:* (Onyx Black) Tsukineko *Chalk ink:* (Charcoal) Clearsnap *Accents:* (black rhinestones) Mark Richards; (copper button) Making Memories *Fibers:* (black ribbon) Michaels *Tool:* (corner rounder punch) Creative Memories

## Classy Celebrate

Designer: Charlene Austin

❶ Make card from cardstock; adhere patterned paper. ❷ Die-cut and emboss label from cardstock, apply rub-on, and adhere. ❸ Tie on ribbon and adhere rhinestones.

*Finished size: 4½" x 6"*

**SUPPLIES:** *Cardstock:* (Vintage Cream) Papertrey Ink *Patterned paper:* (Mud Mask from Origins collection) BasicGrey *Accents:* (clear rhinestones) Queen & Co. *Rub-on:* (celebrate) American Crafts *Fibers:* (yellow ribbon) Papertrey Ink *Die:* (label) Spellbinders

### Butterflies on Green

Designer: Jessica Witty

1 Make card from cardstock. 2 Ink edges heavily.
3 Stamp butterflies and Birthday Wishes.

*Finished size: 5¼" x 4"*

### Pink & Green Friend

Designer: Teri Anderson

1 Make card from cardstock; adhere patterned paper. 2 Trim patterned paper and adhere. 3 Mat strip of patterned paper with cardstock, affix circle sticker, and adhere. 4 Print "friend" on cardstock, trim, and adhere using foam tape. 5 Adhere ribbon and pearls.

*Finished size: 4¼" x 5½"*

**SUPPLIES:** *Cardstock:* (white) Papertrey Ink *Rubber stamp:* (Birthday Wishes) Rubbernecker Stamp Co. *Clear stamps:* (butterflies from Butterfly set) Martha Stewart Crafts *Dye ink:* (Black Soot) Ranger Industries *Chalk ink:* (Lime Pastel) Clearsnap

**SUPPLIES:** *Cardstock:* (hot pink) WorldWin; (white) Bazzill Basics Paper *Patterned paper:* (green circles, green monochromatic, pink monochromatic from Isabelle collection) Anna Griffin *Accents:* (white pearls) Zva Creative *Sticker:* (green circle) Anna Griffin *Fibers:* (pink ribbon) *Font:* (Jane Austen) www.dafont.com

## Quilted Best Wishes

Designer: Alicia Thelin

❶ Make card from cardstock. ❷ Die-cut label from cardstock piece to create frame. Layer bottom to top: scrap cardstock, batting, fabric, frame. *Note: Fabric should puff up through frame.* ❸ Zigzag-stitch around inside edge of frame. ❹ Die-cut label from cardstock piece to create additional frame; adhere to layered panel. Trim excess fabric from around frame and attach brads. ❺ Tie on ribbon. Stamp best wishes on cardstock, trim, and adhere. Attach clip. ❻ Adhere panel to card.

*Finished size: 4½" x 5½"*

## Traditional Joy

Designer: Windy Robinson

❶ Make card from cardstock; cover with patterned paper. ❷ Trim cardstock panel, mat with cardstock, and adhere. ❸ Fold ribbon pleats and adhere. ❹ Tie ribbon bow, adhere, and attach corsage pins. ❺ Stamp sentiment on cardstock, trim into tag, and adhere. ❻ Adhere button and pearl.

*Finished size: 4¼" x 5½"*

**SUPPLIES:** All supplies from Stampin' Up! unless otherwise noted. *Cardstock:* (So Saffron, white); (lime green) Die Cuts With a View *Rubber stamp:* (best wishes from Short & Sweet set) *Dye ink:* (Basic Black) *Accents:* (silver brads, black clip) *Fibers:* (red ribbon) *Die:* (label) *Other:* (black damask fabric, quilting batting) no source

**SUPPLIES:** *Cardstock:* (white) Bazzill Basics Paper *Patterned paper:* (Peppermint Twist from Eskimo Kisses collection) BasicGrey *Clear stamp:* (joy from Small Christmas Phrases set) Martha Stewart Crafts *Specialty ink:* (red hybrid) Technique Tuesday *Accents:* (white button) Blumenthal Lansing; (red corsage pins) Prym-Dritz; (red pearl) Kaisercraft *Fibers:* (red ribbon) Wrights; (white ribbon) Offray

## Birdcage Thank You

Designer: Rae Barthel

❶ Make card from cardstock. ❷ Adhere patterned paper.
❸ Apply rub-on to patterned paper panel and mat with
cardstock. ❹ Tie on ribbon and adhere using foam tape.

*Finished size: 6" x 4"*

## Thank You Butterfly

Designer: Betsy Veldman

❶ Make card from cardstock; punch edge of card front. Adhere
patterned paper inside card. ❷ Cut panel from patterned paper;
mat with cardstock. ❸ Stamp sentiment on cardstock, adhere to
panel, and stitch edges. Adhere panel with foam tape. ❹ Die-cut
frame from felt and adhere; die-cut three butterflies from cardstock
and stamp butterflies on each; color. ❺ Fold butterfles in half for
dimension and adhere wings together; adhere to card.

*Finished size: 4¼" x 5½"*

**SUPPLIES:** *Cardstock:* (Avalanche) Bazzill Basics Paper *Patterned paper:* (Belle Rose,
Salon les Fleur from Postcards from Paris collection) Webster's Pages
*Rub-on:* (thank you) Crate Paper *Fibers:* (white ribbon) Papertrey Ink

**SUPPLIES:** *Cardstock:* (Aqua Mist, Ripe Avocado, white) Papertrey Ink *Patterned
paper:* (Birds of Paradise from Everblooming collection) Kaisercraft *Clear stamps:*
(butterfly from Butterfly Dreams set; sentiment from Damask Designs set) Papertrey
Ink *Specialty ink:* (Noir hybrid) Stewart Superior Corp. *Color medium:* (olive, aqua,
teal markers) Copic *Accents:* (white pearls) Melissa Frances *Dies:* (frame, butterfly)
Papertrey Ink *Tools:* (border punch) Fiskars *Other:* (black felt) Papertrey Ink

**DESIGNER TIP**

Add an unexpected embellishment, such as a single black rhinestone in a row of clear rhinestones for a polished look.

## Be Mine

Designer: Maile Belles

❶ Make card from cardstock. ❷ Cut cardstock square; stamp flourishes and sentiment; round corners and adhere with foam tape. ❸ Stamp heart on cardstock; emboss. Cut out and adhere with foam tape. ❹ Adhere rhinestones.

*Finished size: 5" square*

**SUPPLIES:** *Cardstock:* (Pink Shimmer, white) Papertrey Ink *Clear stamps:* (heart from Heart Prints set, flourish from Fancy Flourishes set) Papertrey Ink; (sentiment from Love Birds set) Wplus9 Design Studio *Pigment ink:* (Sweet Blush) Papertrey Ink *Watermark ink:* Tsukineko *Specialty ink:* (True Black hybrid) Papertrey Ink *Embossing powder:* (black) Jo-Ann Stores *Accents:* (clear, black rhinestones) Hero Arts *Tool:* (corner rounder punch) EK Success

## Pink & Black Just Because

Designer: Charlene Austin

❶ Make card from cardstock. ❷ Paint cardstock block, stamp flower repeatedly, and mat with cardstock. ❸ Border-punch cardstock, trim, and adhere. ❹ Stitch edges and adhere panel. ❺ Adhere cardstock strip, stamp sentiment, and adhere flourish. ❻ Adhere flower and rhinestone.

*Finished size: 5½" square*

**SUPPLIES:** *Cardstock:* (True Black, Vintage Cream) Papertrey Ink *Clear stamps:* (just because, flower from Giga Guide Lines set) Papertrey Ink *Pigment ink:* (Vintage Cream) Papertrey Ink *Paint:* (light pink) *Accents:* (clear rhinestone flourish, clear rhinestone) Westrim Crafts; (black crocheted flower) *Tool:* (embossing border punch) EK Success

## Hanukkah

Designer: Jessica Witty

1 Make card from cardstock. 2 Cut vellum to fit card front, emboss, and adhere. 3 Emboss strip of glitter cardstock, adhere to cardstock panel, and mat with cardstock. 4 Spell "Hanukkah" with stickers. 5 Adhere panel using foam tape.

*Finished size: 4" x 5½"*

**SUPPLIES:** *Cardstock:* (Enchanted Evening, Soft Sky, white) Papertrey Ink; (silver glitter) Best Creation *Vellum:* Papertrey Ink *Stickers:* (Diva Shimmer alphabet) Making Memories *Templates:* (Swiss Dots, Organic Flourish embossing) Provo Craft

## Mother

Designer: Dawn McVey

1 Make card from cardstock. 2 Cut cardstock; stamp background, round bottom corners, and adhere. 3 Cut panel of cardstock; stamp mother and sentiment. Round bottom corners. 4 Tie on ribbon; adhere button and adhere to card with foam tape.

*Finished size: 5½" x 4¼"*

**SUPPLIES:** *Cardstock:* (Vintage Cream, Berry Sorbet) Papertrey ink *Rubber stamp:* (Antique Flower Background) Hero Arts *Clear stamps:* (mother, sentiment from Mother set) Papertrey Ink *Specialty ink:* (Berry Sorbet, Smokey Shadow hybrid) Papertrey Ink *Accent:* (pink button) Papertrey Ink *Fibers:* (cream striped ribbon) Papertrey Ink *Tool:* (corner rounder punch) We R Memory Keepers

**DESIGNER TIP**

Stretch your supplies by thinking of unusual ways to use them. The pearls on this card were actually part of an adhesive accent. By cutting it into sections, you can "straighten" the swirl to make a great ribbon topper.

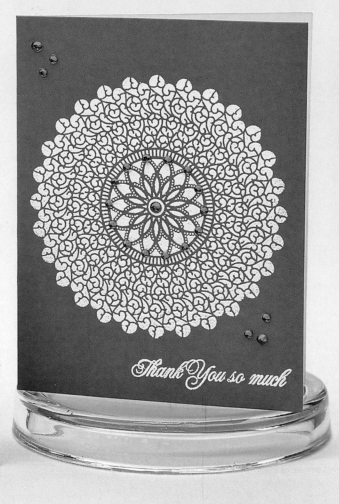

## 5 STEPS Your Kindness

Designer: Beth Opel

**1** Make card from cardstock **2** Print sentiment on card. *Note: Decorative bar is part of font.* **3** Trim and adhere patterned paper. **4** Adhere ribbon. **5** Adhere pearls.

*Finished size: 5½" x 4"*

## 5 STEPS Doily Thank You

Designer: Vanessa Menhorn

**1** Stamp lace and sentiment on card; emboss.
**2** Adhere rhinestones.

*Finished size: 4¼" x 5½"*

**SUPPLIES:** *Cardstock:* (ivory) American Crafts *Patterned paper:* (Collector's Item from The Thrift Shop collection) October Afternoon *Accents:* (silver pearls) Zva Creative *Fibers:* (ivory pleated ribbon) Making Memories *Fonts:* (Kreider) Chatterbox; (Caslon Open Face BT) www.fonts.com; (Seperates) www.myfonts.com

**SUPPLIES:** *Rubber stamp:* (Starburst Lace) Hero Arts *Clear stamp:* (sentiment from Damask Designs) Papertrey Ink *Watermark ink:* Tsukineko *Embossing powder:* (white) Ranger Industries *Accents:* (teal rhinestones) Hero Arts *Other:* (gray card) Hero Arts

# Shabby Chic & Vintage

Shabby chic is a style characterized by layering. It is soft, utilizing ribbon, lace, and techniques such as inking and distressing. The final product looks comfortable, weathered, and worn.

Vintage is characterized by many of the same qualities as shabby chic, but it goes a step further by adding old images, found items, and antique trinkets to the mix. In addition to incorporating time-worn layers of lace and glitter, the vintage style takes us back through time, giving us a connection to our heritage.

## DESIGNER TIP

To tone down brightly colored papers and give them more of a shabby feel, apply cream or white paint to the edges or all over for a faded whitewash effect.

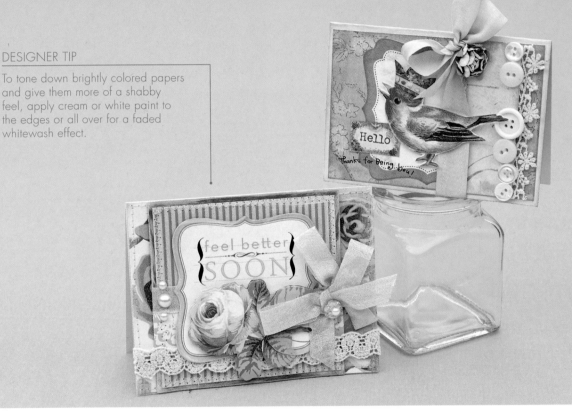

## Floral Feel Better

Designer: Anabelle O'Malley

❶ Make card from cardstock. ❷ Trim patterned paper to fit card front; dry-brush edges with paint, stitch, ink, and adhere. ❸ Trim patterned paper panel; paint and zigzag-stitch edges. Mat with cardstock; paint edges. Affix border sticker. ❹ Tie ribbon around panel and adhere to card. Adhere lace. ❺ Apply rub-on to journaling card; paint edges and adhere. Affix rose sticker. ❻ Adhere button and pearls.

*Finished size: 5½" x 4¼"*

**SUPPLIES:** *Cardstock:* (white) Creative Imaginations *Patterned paper:* (Rose, Patsy from Botanique collection) American Crafts *Dye ink:* (Chamomile) Papertrey Ink *Paint:* (ivory) Delta *Accents:* (green journaling card) Anna Griffin; (cream pearls) Zva Creative; (pink button) *Rub-on:* (sentiment) American Crafts *Stickers:* (rose, tan damask border) Anna Griffin *Fibers:* (pink ribbon) Caramelos; (ivory lace) Michaels

## Thanks for Being You

Designer: Melissa Phillips

❶ Make card from cardstock. ❷ Trim patterned paper, paint edges, and adhere. Ink edges of journaling label and adhere. ❸ Adhere trim. Cut patterned paper strip; ink edges and adhere. Adhere buttons. ❹ Tie on ribbon and adhere flower. ❺ Fussy-cut bird, crown, and hello; adhere. *Note: Use foam tape for bird and crown.* ❻ Apply sentiment rub-on.

*Finished size: 5" x 3¾"*

**SUPPLIES:** *Cardstock:* (Aqua Mist) Papertrey Ink *Patterned paper:* (Maxine from Vintage Posey collection; Anastasia from Attic Treasures collection) Melissa Frances *Dye ink:* (Old Paper) Ranger Industries *Paint:* (Antique White) Delta *Accents:* (pink flower) Prima; (ivory buttons) Papertrey Ink; (cardstock bird, crown, hello) Crafty Secrets; (pink journaling label) Anna Griffin *Rub-on:* (sentiment) Melissa Frances *Fibers:* (tan twill) Wrights; (ivory trim) Prima

DESIGNER TIP

When adhering patterned paper to chipboard, flip it over and trace it on the back for a perfect fit. Sand and ink the edges for an even shabbier look.

BONUS IDEA

Instead of using a full flower, fold an even larger flower in half for the bird's wing.

## Cameo Birthday

Designer: Anabelle O'Malley

❶ Cut patterned paper panel to fit card front; paint and stitch edges. ❷ Cut label; paint edges and adhere to panel. ❸ Adhere ribbons and trim. Adhere roses die cut with foam tape. ❹ Apply rub-on to patterned paper; trim. Adhere happy birthday and adhere to panel with foam tape. ❺ Adhere panel to card. Adhere cameo and pearls.

*Finished size: 4¼" x 5½"*

**SUPPLIES:** *Patterned paper:* (In Due Time from Lullaby Lane collection) Webster's Pages *Paint:* (ivory) Delta *Accents:* (label die cut, cameo) Webster's Pages; (vintage roses die cut) Mamelok Press; (happy birthday) Crafty Secrets *Rub-on:* (gold label) Hambly Screen Prints *Fibers:* (gold mesh, peach ribbon) Webster's Pages; (cream trim) *Other:* (white card) Creative Imaginations

## Peachy Hello

Designer: Anabelle O'Malley

❶ Make card from cardstock; ink and stitch edges. ❷ Affix label; Adhere lace and trim; tie ribbon around card front. Thread button with twine and tie to ribbon. ❸ Adhere patterned paper to bird; trim, sand, and ink edges. Adhere leaf for wing and button and bead for eye. Adhere bird with foam tape. ❹ Replace flower center with button and adhere. ❺ Stamp hello on cardstock; trim and ink edges. Adhere.

*Finished size: 4¼" x 4½"*

**SUPPLIES:** *Cardstock:* (Vintage Cream) Papertrey Ink *Patterned paper:* (Apron Strings from Farmer's Wife collection) Jenni Bowlin Studio *Clear stamp:* (hello from Beyond Basic Borders set) Papertrey Ink *Dye ink:* (Antique Linen) Ranger Industries *Specialty ink:* (Enchanted Evening hybrid) Papertrey Ink *Accents:* (chipboard bird) Jenni Bowlin Studio; (orange flower) Prima; (ivory, peach buttons) Papertrey Ink; (silver bead trim) Darice; (silver leaf) Caramelos *Sticker:* (orange polka dot label) Jenni Bowlin Studio *Fibers:* (ivory lace) May Arts; (cream stitched ribbon, ivory twine) Papertrey Ink

DESIGNER TIP

Mixing up different button styles enhances the shabby look.

## ⟨5 STEPS⟩ Believe

Designer: Julia Stainton

❶ Make card from cardstock. ❷ Adhere patterned paper pieces; ink edges. ❸ Die-cut star from patterned paper; ink edges and adhere. Adhere fabric label and stitch edges. ❹ Paint chipboard holly; adhere. ❺ Adhere buttons, threading with twine as desired.

*Finished size: 4¼" x 5½"*

## ⟨5 STEPS⟩ Birthday Girl Cupcake

Designer: Melissa Phillips

❶ Make card from cardstock; paint edges. ❷ Cut patterned paper panel; stamp sentiment and ink edges. Adhere patterned paper and sheet music strips; adhere panel to card. ❸ Ink ribbon; tie on. Ink edges of trim and adhere. ❹ Cover cupcake bottom and middle with patterned paper, sand and ink edges, and adhere. Paint cupcake top, zigzag-stitch, and adhere glitter; adhere. ❺ Thread button with twine, adhere to flower, and adhere to card.

*Finished size: 4" x 5"*

**SUPPLIES:** *Cardstock:* (white) Cornish Heritage Farms *Patterned paper:* (Christmas Sky from Home for the Holidays collection; Snowflakes & Feathers, Snow Tips from Winter's Wings collection) Webster's Pages *Dye ink:* (Brushed Corduroy) Ranger Industries *Paint:* (Picket Fence crackle) Ranger Industries *Accents:* (believe fabric label) Webster's Pages; (white, cream buttons) Melissa Frances; (chipboard holly) Tim Holtz *Fibers:* (brown, jute twine) *Die:* (star) Spellbinders

**SUPPLIES:** *Cardstock:* (kraft) Papertrey Ink *Patterned paper:* (Tiptoe, Faith from Flights of Fancy collection) Prima; (I'm Yours from Vintage Valentine collection) Fancy Pants Designs *Clear stamp:* (sentiment from Butterfly Dreams set) Papertrey Ink *Dye ink:* (Old Paper) Ranger Industries *Specialty ink:* (Smokey Shadow hybrid) Papertrey Ink *Paint:* (Antique White) Delta *Accents:* (chipboard cupcake) Maya Road; (white glitter) Doodlebug Design; (pink button) Papertrey Ink; (ivory flower) *Fibers:* (cream trim) Prima; (blue ribbon) MemrieMare *Other:* (vintage sheet music)

## Shabby Thank You

Designer: Lisa Dorsey

❶ Make card from cardstock. ❷ Cut patterned paper panel; distress edges, adhere lace, and adhere to card. ❸ Die-cut label from chipboard and cardstock; adhere together. Print "Thank you" on patterned paper; die-cut into label. Trim slightly smaller, ink edges, mat with first label, and adhere to card. ❹ Adhere rhinestones and affix flourish. Attach brad to flower and adhere. Attach brad. ❺ Cut cardstock circle and adhere tulle to create flower. Attach brad and adhere to card.

*Finished size: 5" x 4"*

## Vintage Wishes

Designer: Sherry Wright

*Ink all edges.*

❶ Make card from patterned paper; cover with patterned paper. ❷ Cut patterned paper piece; spray with ink and adhere. ❸ Trim patterned paper panel, distress edges, and adhere. ❹ Spray frame with ink; adhere. Stamp sentiment on cardstock, spray with ink, and adhere. ❺ Adhere flourish and flowers.

*Finished size: 4¼" x 5½"*

**SUPPLIES:** *Cardstock:* (gray) Bazzill Basics Paper; (pink) *Patterned paper:* (Tea Box Primrose from Lotus collection) K&Company; (Cream Sweet Pea from French Sweet Pea collection) Creative Imaginations *Chalk ink:* (black) Clearsnap *Accents:* (vintage brads) Creative Charms; (pink flower) Prima; (clear rhinestones) Michaels *Sticker:* (blue glitter chipboard swirl) Making Memories *Fibers:* (white vintage lace) Melissa Frances; (pink tulle) *Font:* (Edwardian) www.fonts.com *Die:* (label) Ellison *Other:* (chipboard)

**SUPPLIES:** *Cardstock:* (ivory) *Patterned paper:* (Coffee Dot from Double Dot collection) BoBunny Press; (Dress Pattern, Red Floral from Vintage Findings collection) Making Memories *Clear stamp:* (sentiment from Mega Mixed Messages set) Papertrey Ink *Chalk ink:* (Chestnut Roan) Clearsnap *Specialty ink:* (Sherbet, Twilight shimmer spray) Tattered Angels *Accents:* (pink, blue flowers; blue pearl flourish) Zva Creative; (chipboard frame) Tattered Angels

BONUS IDEA
Try this same basic design idea with
other card shapes, like stars or hearts.

## 5 STEPS Sew Glad We're Friends

Designer: Cindy Holshouser

❶ Make card from cardstock; round bottom corners and ink
edges. ❷ Trim and adhere patterned paper piece and strip,
rounding bottom corners of strip. Adhere border across seam.
❸ Scan and print sewing pattern on cardstock; trim and ink
edges. Adhere. ❹ Print sentiment; die-cut into label. Ink edges
and adhere with foam tape. ❺ Die-cut flower from patterned
paper. Thread both buttons with twine and adhere to flower;
adhere flower.

*Finished size: 4" x 5½"*

**SUPPLIES:** *Cardstock:* (Vintage Cream) Papertrey Ink *Patterned paper:* (green floral
from Earthy pad) Crafty Secrets; (red check, blue lined) *Dye ink:* (Antique Linen) Ranger
Industries *Accents:* (white circles border) Creative Imaginations; (red chipboard button)
Jenni Bowlin Studio; (green button) Papertrey Ink *Fibers:* (ivory twine) Papertrey Ink
*Font:* (CK Curly) Creating Keepsakes *Dies:* (label) Spellbinders; (flower) Provo Craft
*Tool:* (corner rounder punch) Fiskars *Other:* (vintage sewing pattern)

## Balloon Love

Designer: Nina Brackett

❶ Adhere doily to cardstock; cut around and ink edges. Cut
cardstock using doily piece as template, score 1" from top, and
adhere behind doily piece to form card. ❷ Trim patterned paper
strip and adhere; zigzag-stitch edges. ❸ Die-cut circle from
patterned paper; ink edges. Mat with die-cut scalloped cardstock
circle. ❹ Stamp sentiment; adhere pearls. Adhere piece with
foam tape. ❺ Stamp butterfly on patterned paper, color with
markers, and cut out. Adhere glitter. Adhere flower and butterfly.
❻ Thread button with string and adhere. Tie ribbon bow and
adhere.

*Finished size: 6" diameter*

**SUPPLIES:** *Cardstock:* (Lipstick Red) Gina K Designs *Patterned paper:* (Tres Magique,
Salon les fleur from Postcards from Paris collection) Webster's Pages *Rubber stamp:*
(sentiment from Warm & Wonderful set) Gina K Designs *Clear stamp:* (butterfly from
Butterfly Collector set) Layers of Color *Dye ink:* (Tuscan Tan, Brick Red) Clearsnap; (Rich
Cocoa) Tsukineko *Color medium:* (green markers) Copic *Accents:* (white flower) Bazzill
Basics Paper; (red button) Gina K Designs; (iridescent glitter) Martha Stewart Crafts;
(white pearls) Mark Richards *Fibers:* (green ribbon, white string) *Dies:*
(circle, scalloped circle) Spellbinders

## Kind Birthday Wishes

Designer: Cindy Holshouser

❶ Make card from cardstock. Cover with patterned paper; stitch edges. ❷ Stamp text on patterned paper; die-cut into label. Trim top and left edge; adhere. ❸ Print sewing pattern image on cardstock; trim, ink edges, and adhere. Adhere glitter. ❹ Stamp sentiment on cardstock; trim, ink edges, and punch. Tie on twine and adhere with foam tape.

*Finished size: 4" x 5½"*

**SUPPLIES:** *Cardstock:* (Vintage Cream) Papertrey Ink *Patterned paper:* (Simple as Pie from Domestic Goddess collection) Graphic 45; (cream ledger from Noteworthy collection notebook) Making Memories *Clear stamps:* (text from Background Basics: Text Style set) Papertrey Ink; (sentiment from Card Sentiments set) Crafty Secrets *Dye ink:* (Antique Linen) Ranger Industries *Specialty ink:* (Smokey Shadow hybrid) Papertrey Ink *Accent:* (iridescent glitter) Hero Arts *Digital image:* (vintage sewing pattern) *Fibers:* (cream twine) Papertrey Ink *Die:* (label) Spellbinders *Tool:* (⅛" circle punch)

## Anniversary Cherubs

Designer: Danielle Flanders

*Paint all paper edges.*

❶ Make card from cardstock. ❷ Cut patterned paper panel; round top corners. Adhere ticket and apply rub-on. ❸ Cut patterned paper piece; adhere. Trim border sticker; affix to cardstock strip and adhere to panel. Zigzag-stitch. ❹ Tie on ribbon, adhere brad, and adhere panel to card. ❺ Cover angels with glitter; adhere to card.

*Finished size: 3½" x 5¼"*

**SUPPLIES:** *Cardstock:* (silver, white) *Patterned paper:* (Front Porch, Trellis from Bayberry Cottage collection) Pink Paislee *Paint:* (white) Delta *Accents:* (blue houndstooth ticket, white glitter) Pink Paislee; (white resin angels) Melissa Frances; (red rhinestone brad) Pink Paislee *Rub-on:* (forever) Melissa Frances *Sticker:* (clear flourish border) Pink Paislee *Fibers:* (gray ribbon) *Tool:* (corner rounder punch)

**DESIGNER TIP**
Find old books at garage sales or thrift shops, or make a new book page look aged by inking or painting the edges.

## Six Button Thanks

Designer: Danielle Flanders

① Apply background rub-ons to card; zigzag-stitch. ② Apply butterfly and sentiment rub-ons. ③ Thread twine through buttons, knot ends, and adhere.

*Finished size: 5¼" x 4"*

## Muted Sympathy

Designer: Anabelle O'Malley

① Make card from cardstock. ② Trim book page; paint edges and adhere. Stitch edges. ③ Trim patterned paper strip; paint edges and adhere. Zigzag-stitch one edge. ④ Stamp with sympathy on cardstock, trim and adhere. Adhere pearl accent to label holder; adhere label holder. ⑤ Adhere flower. Tie on ribbon.

*Finished size: 4¼" x 5½"*

**SUPPLIES:** *Accents:* (white, cream buttons) Jenni Bowlin Studio *Rub-ons:* (labels, butterfly) Jenni Bowlin Studio; (sentiment) Melissa Frances *Fibers:* (jute twine) *Other:* (kraft card) WorldWin

**SUPPLIES:** *Cardstock:* (ivory) The Paper Company *Patterned paper:* (Celebration from Le' Romantique collection) Graphic 45 *Clear stamp:* (with sympathy from Mega Mixed Messages set) Papertrey Ink *Dye ink:* (Antique Linen) Ranger Industries *Specialty ink:* (True Black hybrid) Papertrey Ink *Paint:* (ivory) Delta *Accents:* (tan flower, brown pearl accent) Prima; (silver label holder) Making Memories *Fibers:* (black/cream striped ribbon) Caramelos *Other:* (vintage book page)

DESIGNER TIP

Sometimes the perfect accent, such as the butterfly on this card, is just a bit too bright and new for the vintage look. Sanding adds age, making the accent look right at home on a vintage card.

## Shabby Thanks

Designer: Sherry Wright

*Ink all edges.*

❶ Make card from cardstock. ❷ Cut patterned paper slightly smaller than card front; adhere. Cut patterned paper piece; adhere. ❸ Adhere lace. Adhere floral card. ❹ Bend vine as desired; adhere to card. ❺ Stamp sentiment on patterned paper; punch into circle and adhere.

*Finished size: 4½" x 5¾"*

## Butterfly Because

Designer: Lisa Dorsey

❶ Make card from cardstock. ❷ Cut sheet music block; ink edges. ❸ Attach brad to tag; ink edges and adhere to block. Affix calendar. ❹ Cut two butterflies from postcards. Sand one butterfly and adhere to second with foam tape. Adhere pearls and adhere to block. ❺ Tie on ribbon; adhere block to card. ❻ Print sentiment on cardstock, trim into tag, and ink edges. Adhere. Thread button with twine and adhere.

*Finished size: 5½" x 5¼"*

**SUPPLIES:** *Cardstock:* (brown) Papertrey Ink *Patterned paper:* (Island Beauty from Paradise collection) Prima; (cream lined from Birds & Botanicals pad) Crafty Secrets *Clear stamp:* (sentiment from Mega Mixed Messages set) Papertrey Ink *Chalk ink:* (Chestnut Roan) Clearsnap *Accents:* (white flower/butterfly vine) Prima; (floral card) Crafty Secrets *Fibers:* (cream lace) Webster's Pages *Tool:* (circle punch) McGill

**SUPPLIES:** *Cardstock:* (brown) Bazzill Basics Paper; (cream) *Dye ink:* (Antique Linen) Ranger Industries *Accents:* (Paris tag) 7gypsies; (butterfly postcard) Cavallini Papers & Co.; (green pearls) Michaels; (vintage rhinestone brad) Creative Charms; (red button) *Stickers:* (calendar) Melissa Frances *Fibers:* (green wired ribbon) Hobby Lobby; (natural twine) May Arts *Font:* (your choice) *Other:* (vintage sheet music)

**DESIGNER TIP**

If you don't have the perfect ribbon color, it's easy to dye ribbon with ink. Place the ribbon in a plastic bag, add a few drops of ink, and rub it into the ribbon. Then remove the ribbon and give it a minute to dry. This is a great way to create soft and aged colors that match your shabby card perfectly.

**BONUS IDEA**

Use a stamp set containing several similarly-themed images, such as the set used here, to create a coordinating set of cards as a gift for a loved one.

## Peach Belle Thanks

Designer: Debbie Olson

❶ Make card from cardstock. ❷ Cut patterned paper slightly smaller than card front; sand edges and adhere. Adhere lace. ❸ Die-cut border from patterned paper strip; sand edges, adhere, and zigzag-stitch. Tie on ribbon. ❹ Stamp scene on cardstock; color and accent with glitter pens. Ink and distress edges, mat with cardstock, and distress mat edges. Adhere to card with foam tape. ❺ Die-cut tag from cardstock; stamp thanks. Ink edges and adhere with foam tape. Thread buttons with floss and adhere.

*Finished size: 4¼" x 5½"*

## Doily Congratulations

Designer: Nina Brackett

❶ Make card from cardstock; ink edges. ❷ Print digital paper on cardstock; trim, ink edges, and adhere. Stitch edges. ❸ Stamp flourish and congratulations. ❹ Adhere doily. Tie on twill; attach brad to button and adhere. ❺ Stamp flowers on cardstock; color with markers, cut out, and adhere, using foam tape for one. ❻ Stamp butterfly, cut out, and adhere. Adhere pearls.

*Finished size: 4¼" x 5½"*

**SUPPLIES:** *Cardstock:* (Vintage Cream, Melon Berry) Papertrey Ink *Patterned paper:* (Pure Grace, peach polka dots from Lullaby Lane & Life's Portrait pad) Webster's Pages *Clear stamps:* (scene from Seasonal Friends set) Crafty Secrets; (thanks from Mega Mixed Messages set) Papertrey Ink *Dye ink:* (Rich Cocoa) Tsukineko; (Chamomile) Papertrey Ink *Specialty ink:* (Melon Berry hybrid) Papertrey Ink *Color media:* (assorted markers; clear, peach, mint glitter pens) Copic *Accents:* (cream, peach, aqua buttons) Papertrey Ink *Fibers:* (cream lace) Prima; (peach ribbon) May Arts; (cream floss) *Dies:* (tag, scalloped border) Spellbinders

**SUPPLIES:** *Cardstock:* (ivory, Innocent Pink) Gina K Designs *Rubber stamp:* (congratulations from Inside & Out set) Gina K Designs *Clear stamps:* (butterfly from Butterfly Collector set; flourish, flowers from Nature Walk set) Layers of Color *Dye ink:* (Tuscan Tan, Tea Rose) Clearsnap; (Rich Cocoa) Tsukineko *Color medium:* (pink markers) Copic *Accents:* (pink glitter brad) Michaels; (peach button) Gina K Designs; (white pearls) Mark Richards; (vellum doily) *Digital element:* (pink houndstooth patterned paper from Swing into Spring kit) Gina K Designs *Fibers:* (brown twill)

## Crossword Dad

Designer: Julia Stainton

*Ink all edges.*

❶ Make card from cardstock. ❷ Cut patterned paper block, distress edges, and adhere. ❸ Stamp Crossword Scrapblock on cardboard piece. Peel away paper layer to reveal corrugated layer. ❹ Spell "Dad" with stickers on piece; attach bookplate. ❺ Wrap twine around piece, affix authentic sticker, and attach safety pin. Adhere piece to card.

*Finished size: 5¼" square*

## Grateful

Designer: Lisa Dorsey

❶ Make card from cardstock. ❷ Trim patterned paper; mat two edges with cardstock and trim with decorative-edge cutter. Ink edges and adhere. ❸ Paint frame; adhere. Thread buttons with twine and adhere. ❹ Cut postcard from patterned paper; adhere with foam tape. Adhere die cut with foam tape. ❺ Adhere trim and flower.

*Finished size: 7" x 4¾"*

**SUPPLIES:** *Cardstock:* (black) Bazzill Basics Paper *Patterned paper:* (In Stitches from Material Girl collection) Cosmo Cricket *Rubber stamp:* (Crossword Scrapblock) Cornish Heritage Farms *Dye ink:* (Brushed Corduroy, black) Ranger Industries *Accents:* (antique brass bookplate, safety pin) Tim Holtz *Stickers:* (Tiny Type alphabet) Cosmo Cricket; (100% authentic) *Fibers:* (natural twine) *Other:* (corrugated cardboard)

**SUPPLIES:** *Cardstock:* (brown) Bazzill Basics Paper; (yellow) *Patterned paper:* (Jacobean Red from Red, Black, & Cream collection) Autumn Leaves; (Postcards from Amber Road collection) Pink Paislee *Dye ink:* (Antique Linen) Ranger Industries *Paint:* (Antique Linen crackle) Ranger Industries *Accents:* (grateful die cut) Pink Paislee; (ivory chipboard button) Jenni Bowlin Studio; (chipboard bracket frame) Magistical Memories; (peach flower) Prima; (teal button) Papertrey Ink *Fibers:* (teal trim) Making Memories; (brown twine) May Arts *Tool:* (decorative-edge rotary cutter) Fiskars

**DESIGNER TIPS**

Use a glue pen to adhere glitter to very small areas.

*Cindy's vintage girl photo came from a CD that accompanies the book Memories of a Lifetime: Florals & Nature: Artwork for Scrapbooks & Fabric-Transfer Crafts.*

## Old-Fashioned Luck

Designer: Cindy Holshouser

*Ink all edges.*

**1** Make card from cardstock. **2** Trim patterned papers and adhere. Adhere lace and zigzag-stitch in place. **3** Apply glitter glue to vintage image; adhere image. **4** Stamp sentiment on cardstock; die-cut into tag and adhere with foam tape. **5** Ink edges of flower; affix rhinestones and adhere.

*Finished size: 3¾" x 5¼"*

**SUPPLIES:** *Cardstock:* (Vintage Cream) Papertrey Ink *Patterned paper:* (cream floral from Earthy pad) Crafty Secrets; (Life Time from Documented collection) Teresa Collins Designs *Clear stamp:* (sentiment from Wishing You set) Papertrey Ink *Dye ink:* (Red Pepper, Antique Linen) Ranger Industries *Accents:* (ivory flower) Michaels; (gold rhinestones) Rhinestones Galore; (pink glitter) Hero Arts *Fibers:* (ivory trim) *Die:* (tag) Spellbinders *Other:* (vintage girl image) Sterling Publishing Co.

## For You

Designer: Julia Stainton

*Ink all edges.*

**1** Make card from cardstock. **2** Cut patterned paper block, mat with patterned paper, and zigzag-stitch seam. Cut patterned paper, distress edges, adhere, and stitch edges. **3** Adhere labels, apply rub-on, and adhere panel to card. **4** Adhere lace. Attach brad to flower and adhere. **5** Spell sentiment with stickers.

*Finished size: 5¼" square*

**SUPPLIES:** *Cardstock:* (kraft) Bazzill Basics Paper *Patterned paper:* (Be Free, Dream Big from 365 Degrees collection) Pink Paislee *Dye ink:* (Brushed Corduroy) Ranger Industries *Accents:* (seeds, cherry labels) Crafty Secrets; (red dotted epoxy brad) Making Memories; (cream flower) Prima *Rub-on:* (bird branch) Jenni Bowlin Studio *Stickers:* (Tiny Type alphabet) Cosmo Cricket; (Rockabye alphabet) American Crafts *Fibers:* (cream lace) Prima

DID YOU KNOW?

Anabelle stamped her sentiment on a blank edge of the sheet music so it would match her card perfectly.

## Antique Anniversary

Designer: Anabelle O'Malley

❶ Make card from patterned paper. ❷ Trim patterned paper panel; paint and stitch edges. ❸ Trim patterned paper and sheet music pieces; paint edges. Adhere to panel, zigzag-stitch. Adhere panel. ❹ Adhere doily. Cut crepe paper strip; stitch one side and gather into rosette. Stitch closed and apply glitter to edges; adhere. ❺ Ink edges of chipboard button; adhere. ❻ Stamp happy anniversary on sheet music; cut out and apply glitter to edges. Adhere. Thread buttons with twine and adhere.

*Finished size: 4" x 5½"*

**SUPPLIES:** *Patterned paper:* (Antique Flowers from Life Stories collection) My Mind's Eye; (Dress Pattern from Vintage Findings collection) Making Memories; (Endeared from Sugared collection) BasicGrey *Specialty paper:* (ivory crepe) Melissa Frances *Clear stamp:* (happy anniversary from Heart Prints set) Papertrey Ink *Dye ink:* (Antique Linen) Ranger Industries *Specialty ink:* (True Black, Pure Poppy hybrid) Papertrey Ink *Paint:* (ivory) Delta *Accents:* (ledger chipboard button) Jenni Bowlin Studio; (gold glitter glue) Ranger Industries; (ivory lace doily, ivory buttons) *Fibers:* (natural twine) Papertrey Ink *Other:* (vintage sheet music)

## :5: Santa Claus is Coming to Town

Designer: Danielle Flanders

❶ Make card from cardstock; punch bottom of card front. ❷ Cut patterned paper, adhere, and zigzag-stitch edges. ❸ Trim journaling card, paint edges, and adhere. Adhere snowflake tag and button. ❹ Paint and distress card edges. Paint bottom of card; let dry and apply sentiment rub-on.

*Finished size: 4" x 4¾"*

**SUPPLIES:** *Patterned paper:* (Honeycomb, Worker Bee from Queen Bee collection) Pink Paislee *Paint:* (white) *Accents:* (journaling card, red cork button) Pink Paislee; (white glitter snowflake tag) Target *Rub-on:* (sentiment) Melissa Frances *Tool:* (border punch) Fiskars

## Vintage Valentine

Designer: Nina Brackett

❶ Make card from cardstock; ink edges. ❷ Trim patterned paper; ink edges and adhere. ❸ Print patterned paper on cardstock; trim. Ink and distress edges; adhere. Stitch three edges. ❹ Adhere lace; tie on ribbon. ❺ Adhere doily. Print vintage valentine on cardstock; trim, ink and distress edges, and adhere with foam tape. Thread buttons with floss and adhere; adhere pearls. ❻ Stamp sentiment on cardstock; trim and round corners. Ink edges and adhere with foam tape.

*Finished size: 4¼" x 5½"*

## Vintage Boo

Designer: Betsy Veldman

❶ Make card from cardstock. ❷ Adhere label; brush edges with paint. Trim cardstock piece; brush edges with paint. ❸ Stamp stars and bat on piece; wrap with twine and adhere to card. ❹ Punch star from cardstock; emboss, ink, and adhere. ❺ Paint chipboard letters; stamp polka dot backgound. Sand edges and adhere. ❻ Thread buttons with twine and adhere.

*Finished size: 4" x 5¾"*

**SUPPLIES:** *Cardstock:* (ivory) Gina K Designs *Patterned paper:* (Merry Berry from Jolly By Golly pad) Cosmo Cricket *Clear stamp:* (sentiment from Damask Designs set) Papertrey Ink *Dye ink:* (Tuscan Tan, Brick Red) Clearsnap *Accents:* (red, pink, ivory buttons) Gina K Designs; (white pearls) Mark Richards; (red heart doily) Hallmark *Digital elements:* (pink butterfly patterned paper from Wings of Hope kit) Gina K Designs; (vintage valentine) graphicsfairy.blogspot.com *Fibers:* (ivory ribbon) Wrights; (ivory floss) DMC; (ivory lace) *Tool:* (corner rounder punch) Fiskars

**SUPPLIES:** *Cardstock:* (Rustic Cream, kraft) Papertrey Ink *Clear stamps:* (bat, star border from Boo to You set; polka dot background from Polka Dot Basics II set) Papertrey Ink *Pigment ink:* (Orange Zest) Papertrey Ink *Chalk ink:* (Creamy Brown) Clearsnap *Specialty ink:* (True Black hybrid) Papertrey Ink *Paint:* (ivory) Delta *Accents:* (New York chipboard alphabet) Maya Road; (orange button) Papertrey Ink; (Halloween canvas label) Pink Paislee; (ivory button) *Fibers:* (ivory, natural twine) Papertrey Ink *Template:* (Polka Dots embossing) Provo Craft *Tool:* (star punch) Fiskars

# Stamping Basics

## INK

### Dye ink
Dries quickly, is translucent, non-toxic, and washable (except for the archival type) and works well for detailed stamps, glossy paper and vellum. It will fade with time and exposure.

### Pigment ink
Dries slowly, is opaque, vivid and fade resistant. Some varieties can be used to stamp on different surface types like wood, glass or fabric, so experiment with it! Its viscosity and slower drying time make it the right choice for heat embossing with powders.

### Solvent ink
Quick drying, opaque, and works well on slick surfaces (such as glossy paper or a transparency) or where a permanent ink is important.

### Hybrid ink
A combination of dye and pigment properties for a wide variety of applications.

## STAMPS

### Clear
Provide ease of image placement, are cost-effective, and require relatively little space to store. A clear acrylic block is needed for best results.

### Red rubber
Provide excellent impression quality, available mounted on cling foam and requiring an acrylic block, or permanently mounted on wood. Cling foam mounted stamps are sometimes offered in a large sheet that requires trimming into individual images.

## CARE AND STORAGE

### Stamps
Clear and cling foam rubber stamps can be placed in CD jewel cases, 3-ring binders with special insert sheets, or clip and spinner systems. Wood-mounted rubber stamps should be stored with the rubber facing up to protect the stamping surface. Clean with a gentle wipe (pop-up baby wipes are handy) or water; air dry.

### Ink
Should be stored with the pad surface facing down so ink remains at the surface of the pad while not in use. Pads can be stacked to optimize space.

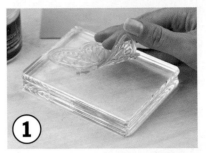

**1** Ink flat side of butterfly stamp; stamp on cardstock and emboss multiple times.

**2** Stamp butterfly on warm embossing powder; let cool.

**3** Trim butterfly and adhere to card.

## Glad to See You Sunshine Card

**Designer:** Jessica Witty

1. Make card from cardstock; stamp Wood Grain Background.
2. Create stamped element, following figures 1–3. Repeat for remaining butterflies.
3. Stamp sentiment.

*Finished size: 5" x 3½"*

**SUPPLIES:** *Rubber stamp:* (Wood Grain Background) Plaid *Clear stamps:* (sentiment from Awesome Days of Summer set) Technique Tuesduy; (butterflies from Butterfly set) Martha Stewart Crafts *Dye ink:* (Early Espresso) Stampin' Up! *Watermark ink:* Tsukineko *Embossing powder:* (Mustard) American Crafts *Cardstock:* (New Leaf, white) Papertrey Ink

DESIGNER TIP

This technique can be used with any symmetrical clear stamp. Just think of the back side of your stamp as a bonus image!

1. Stamp images on watercolor paper, emboss, and apply dye ink.

2. Apply remaining dye ink to create gradient effect, blending with brush as needed.

3. Combine pigment powder and water; spritz on with spray bottle.

## 5 steps · Sunflower Birthday Card
**Designer:** Agata Pfister

1. Make card from cardstock; tie on ribbon bow.
2. Trim specialty paper into rectangle and round corners.
3. Create stamped element, following figures 1–3. Stamp sentiment.
4. Adhere rhinestone and beads. Adhere to card with foam tape.

*Finished size: 6" x 4"*

**SUPPLIES:** *Clear stamps:* (bulls eye, small flowers, petals from Funky Flowers set; happy birthday from Everyday Lines set) My Stamp Box *Dye ink:* (Mustard Seed, Spiced Marmalade, Rusty Hinge, Walnut Stain) Ranger Industries *Solvent ink:* (Jet Black) Tsukineko *Watermark ink:* Tsukineko *Embossing powder:* (white) *Cardstock:* (white) *Specialty paper:* (white watercolor) Canson *Color medium:* (iridescent pigment powder) Ranger Industries *Accents:* (clear rhinestone) Hero Arts; (brown beads) *Fibers:* (white ribbon) *Tool:* (corner rounder punch) EK Success *Other:* (spray bottle) Ranger Industries

**1** Stamp leaf on cardstock with watermark ink.

**2** Sprinkle with embossing powder, shaking off excess.

**3** Emboss using heat tool.

## **5** Congrats Leaf Card

**Designer: Teri Anderson**

1 Make card from cardstock; cover with cardstock.

2 Mat cardstock square with cardstock; adhere to card.

3 Create stamped element, following figures 1–3. Trim image and adhere.

4 Stamp congrats; emboss. Adhere pearls.

*Finished size: 5" square*

### DESIGNER TIP

Rub cardstock with a dryer sheet before stamping and embossing. This keeps stray powder from sticking to your cardstock.

**SUPPLIES:** *Clear stamps:* (congrats from Sentimentally Yours set) Technique Tuesday; (leaf from Turning a New Leaf set) Papertrey Ink *Watermark ink:* Tsukineko *Embossing powder:* (Copper, Silver) American Crafts *Cardstock:* (Rustic Cream) Papertrey Ink; (Charlie metallic) Bazzill Basics Paper; (cream) Georgia-Pacific *Accents:* (white pearls) Zva Creative

Stamp Rose Background on oval; color with ink (see Designer Tip).

Ink edges and apply ultra thick embossing powder; emboss and let cool.

Crack piece by slightly bending edges.

## Vintage Medallion Card

Designer: Vanessa Menhorn

1. Make card from cardstock; adhere patterned paper.
   *Note: Ink edges before adhering.*
2. Adhere ribbon and button.
3. Die-cut oval and scalloped oval from cardstock. Adhere scalloped oval.
4. Create stamped element, following figures 1–3. Ink cracks and adhere.
5. Stamp sentiment and adhere pearls.
6. Tie ribbon bow and adhere.

*Finished size: 4¼" x 5½"*

### DESIGNER TIP

Mix dye ink with water and apply to image using a small paint brush for a fun watercolor look.

**SUPPLIES:** *Rubber stamp:* (Rose Background) Hero Arts *Clear stamp:* (sentiment from Delightful Dahlia set) Papertrey Ink *Dye ink:* (Tuxedo Black) Tsukineko; (Antique Linen, Walnut Stain, Old Paper, Peeled Paint, Worn Lipstick, Spun Sugar) Ranger Industries *Watermark ink:* Tsukineko *Embossing powder:* (clear) Ranger Industries *Cardstock:* (Charlie metallic) Bazzill Basics Paper; (cream) *Patterned paper:* (Dream Big from 365 Degrees collection) Pink Paislee *Accents:* (green button) Papertrey Ink; (cream pearls) Kaisercraft *Fibers:* (pink ribbon) Papertrey Ink *Dies:* (oval, scalloped oval) Spellbinders

DESIGNER TIP
The Sand Dunes Queue from Clearsnap includes six coordinating colors that work perfectly for Trinh's sunset panel.

## :5: Pumpkin Give Thanks Card

**Designer: Maile Belles**

1. Make card from cardstock.

2. Stamp pumpkin squares on cardstock; emboss. Trim and adhere with foam tape.

3. Stamp give thanks and adhere buttons.

*Finished size: 4" square*

## :5: Heartfelt Sympathy Card

**Designer: Trinh Arrieta**

1. Make card from cardstock; round bottom corners.

2. Stamp tree square on cardstock; emboss. Apply ink. Trim and adhere piece with foam tape.

3. Stamp sentiment.

*Finished size: 3½" x 5"*

**SUPPLIES:** All supplies from Papertrey Ink unless otherwise noted. *Clear stamps:* (give thanks, pumpkin squares from Take Three: Fall set) *Pigment ink:* (Fresh Snow) *Specialty ink:* (Dark Chocolate hybrid) *Embossing powder:* (white) Jo-Ann Stores *Cardstock:* (Simply Chartreuse, Harvest Gold, Summer Sunrise, Orange Zest) *Accents:* (brown buttons)

**SUPPLIES:** *Clear stamps:* (tree square, sentiment from Through the Trees set) Papertrey Ink *Chalk ink:* (Sand Dunes Queue) Clearsnap *Embossing powder:* (white) Stampendous! *Cardstock:* (white) The Angel Company *Tool:* (corner rounder punch) We R Memory Keepers

DESIGNER TIP
Use foam tape in varying thicknesses to achieve a multi-dimensional look.

## 5 All Boy Card
**Designer:** Kalyn Kepner

1. Make card from cardstock.
2. Round left corners of cardstock rectangle. Adhere patterned paper strip; trim with decorative-edge scissors. Adhere scalloped border. Adhere panel to card.
3. Stamp airplane and clouds on cardstock; emboss. Trim and adhere with foam tape.
4. Stamp all boy; emboss.

*Finished size: 5½" x 3¾"*

## 5 Motorcycle Dad Tag
**Designer:** Kelley Eubanks

*Ink all paper edges.*

1. Die-cut tag from cardstock.
2. Stamp Motorcycle on patterned paper panel; emboss.
3. Stamp "Dad" on panel. Distress edges and adhere dots. Adhere to tag.
4. Tie on twine bow.

*Finished size: 3½" x 5½"*

**SUPPLIES:** *Clear stamps:* (clouds, airplane from Up Up & Away set) We R Memory Keepers; (all boy from Daily Designs Sentiments set) Papertrey Ink *Watermark ink:* Tsukineko *Chalk ink:* (Ice Blue) Clearsnap *Embossing powder:* (yellow, red, blue, clear) Hampton Art *Cardstock:* (white, blue) Bazzill Basics Paper *Patterned paper:* (Super Stripes from Alphabet Soup Boy collection) My Mind's Eye *Accent:* (red scalloped border) My Mind's Eye *Tools:* (decorative-edge scissors) Fiskars; (corner rounder punch)

**SUPPLIES:** *Rubber stamp:* (Motorcycle) Stampin' Up! *Clear stamps:* (Fresh Alphabet) Papertrey Ink *Dye ink:* (Vintage Photo) Ranger Industries; (Tuxedo Black) Tsukineko *Watermark ink:* Tsukineko *Embossing powder:* (blue) American Crafts *Cardstock:* (kraft) Papertrey Ink *Patterned paper:* (ledger from Library Ledger collection) Papertrey Ink *Accents:* (gold dots) Wilton *Fibers:* (natural jute twine) May Arts *Die:* (tag) Papertrey Ink

DESIGNER TIP

When heat embossing on dark colored cardstock, stamp with white ink and emboss with white powder for a crisper look.

## :5: So Much Chandelier Card

**Designer: Maile Belles**

❶ Make card from cardstock. Die-cut label from cardstock, stamp sentiment, and adhere.

❷ Stamp Chandelier on cardstock rectangle; emboss.

❸ Adhere rhinestones, tie on ribbon bow, and adhere to card with foam tape.

*Finished size: 4¼" x 5½"*

## :5: Special Doily Card

**Designer: Jen Shears**

❶ Make card from cardstock.

❷ Stamp doily on cardstock rectangle; emboss. Spritz with shimmer spray.

❸ Stamp sentiment on panel, distress edges, stitch, and adhere to card.

❹ Tie on ribbon bow. Tie button to card with ribbon.

*Finished size: 5½" x 4¼"*

**SUPPLIES:** *Rubber stamp:* (Chandelier) Hero Arts *Clear stamp:* (sentiment from Damask Designs set) Papertrey Ink *Pigment ink:* (Fresh Snow) Papertrey Ink *Specialty ink:* (Scarlet Jewel hybrid) Papertrey Ink *Embossing powder:* (white) Jo-Ann Stores *Cardstock:* (Scarlet Jewel, kraft, white) Papertrey Ink *Accents:* (yellow rhinestones) K&Company *Fibers:* (yellow ribbon) Papertrey Ink *Die:* (label) Papertrey Ink

**SUPPLIES:** *Clear stamps:* (sentiment from Embellishments set) Papertrey Ink; (doily from The Thrift Shop set) October Afternoon *Watermark ink:* Tsukineko *Specialty ink:* (Smokey Shadow hybrid) Papertrey Ink; (Vintage Pink shimmer spray) Tattered Angels *Embossing powder:* (white) *Cardstock:* (Vintage Cream) Papertrey Ink *Accent:* (cream button) Jenni Bowlin Studio *Fibers:* (pink ribbon) May Arts

**DESIGNER TIP**

This versatile project can be used for a variety of occasions. It's also a fun way to personalize party décor for those hard-to-find occasions.

**DESIGNER TIP**

For best results, place inked stamp face up on the table and roll the pencil across the image.

## 5 STEPS Hanukkah Napkins

**Designer:** Ivanka Lentle

1. Fold napkins.
2. Stamp menorah on napkins; emboss.
3. Tie on ribbon.

*Finished size: 2¾" x 8"*

## 5 STEPS Back to School Pencils

**Designer:** Kim Hughes

1. Stamp sentiment, math equation, and flowers on pencils; emboss.

*Finished size: ¼" diameter x 7¼" long*

**SUPPLIES:** *Clear stamp:* (menorah from Hanukkah set) Studio G  *Pigment ink:* (blue metallic) Maya Road  *Embossing powder:* (clear) Hero Arts  *Fibers:* (teal ribbon) Offray  *Other:* (white napkins) IKEA

**SUPPLIES:** *Rubber stamps:* (sentiment, math equation, flowers from Teacher Fhiona set) Your Next Stamp  *Watermark ink:* Ranger Industries  *Embossing powder:* (Pewter, Rouge, white) American Crafts  *Other:* (pencils)

**1** Stamp butterflies on patterned paper.

**2** Color butterflies with yellow and orange markers.

**3** Accent butterflies with red marker.

## Botanical Sympathy Card

Designer: Betsy Veldman

*Ink all paper edges.*

**1** Make card from cardstock.

**2** Create stamped element, following figures 1–3. Trim piece and adhere. Stamp floral diamonds and round right corners.

**3** Adhere patterned paper strips and affix sticker. Zigzag-stitch seam.

**4** Stamp flowers on card; color with markers. Stamp postage cancellation.

**5** Cut slit in seam, thread twine and tie bow. Thread buttons with twine and adhere.

**6** Stamp oval and with sympathy on patterned paper, trim, and adhere with foam tape.

*Finished size: 4¼" x 5½"*

**SUPPLIES:** *Clear stamps:* (butterflies from Butterfly Dreams set, flowers from Year of Flowers: Gladiolus set, with sympathy from Daily Designs Sentiments set, scripted text from Background Basics: Text Style set, floral diamonds from Background Basics: Botanicals set, oval from Borders & Corners {oval} set) Papertrey Ink; (postage cancellation) Studio Calico *Dye ink:* (Early Espresso) Stampin' Up! *Pigment ink:* (Aqua Mist) Papertrey Ink *Chalk ink:* (Chestnut Roan) Clearsnap *Cardstock:* (Rustic Cream) Papertrey Ink *Patterned paper:* (Cabriole from Curio collection, Glossary from Basics collection) BasicGrey *Color medium:* (red, yellow, orange, green markers) Copic *Accents:* (cream buttons) *Sticker:* (scalloped border) BasicGrey *Fibers:* (natural jute twine) Papertrey Ink *Tool:* (corner rounder punch) EK Success

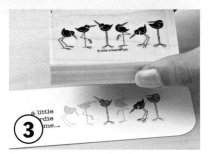

**①** Color birds stamp with markers.

**②** Breathe on stamp to remoisten ink.

**③** Stamp image on cardstock.

## ⁙5⁙ Rainbow Birdie Card

**Designer:** Alicia Thelin

❶ Make card from cardstock.

❷ Create stamped element, following figures 1–3. Trim piece and round right corners.

❸ Stamp sentiment on panel and adhere to card with foam tape.

❹ Thread button with floss and adhere.

❺ Border-punch cardstock and adhere inside front flap.

*Finished size: 5" x 4"*

**SUPPLIES:** All supplies from Stampin' Up! *Rubber stamps:* (sentiment from A Little Birdie Told Me set, birds from Shore Thing set) *Dye ink:* (Basic Black) *Cardstock:* (Whisper White, Tempting Turquoise) *Color medium:* (assorted markers) *Accent:* (white button) *Fibers:* (black floss) *Tools:* (border, corner rounder punches)

DESIGNER TIPS

Inking stamps with markers is a simple way to use lots of colors without masking or creating an inky mess.

If you are right handed, ink your stamp from left to right to avoid smudging the image with your hand.

**1** Stamp pumpkins with leaves on die cut. Color tops and bottoms of pumpkins with markers and gel pen.

**2** Color leaves and stems with markers.

**3** Color acorns with markers and glitter pen.

## Thankful for You Card

**Designer:** Julie Campbell

1. Make card from cardstock; adhere patterned paper rectangles.
2. Deboss cardstock rectangle and adhere. Tie on twine bow.
3. Die-cut labels from cardstock; ink edges. Create stamped element, following figures 1–3.
4. Adhere piece to card with foam tape.
5. Stamp label and sentiment on die cut label; adhere with foam tape.
6. Thread buttons with twine and adhere.

*Finished size: 5½" x 4¼"*

**SUPPLIES:** *Clear stamps:* (pumpkins with leaves, sentiment, label from Friendship Jar Fall Fillers set) Papertrey Ink *Dye ink:* (Chai, Chamomile) Papertrey Ink; (Basic Black) Stampin' Up! *Chalk ink:* (Dark Brown) Clearsnap *Cardstock:* (Rustic Cream, Dark Chocolate) Papertrey Ink *Patterned paper:* (Recess from Show & Tell collection) We R Memory Keepers; (Open Your Heart Berry Stem from So Sophie collection) My Mind's Eye *Color media:* (purple, orange, brown, green markers; iridescent glitter pen) Copic; (white gel pen) Ranger Industries *Accents:* (wood buttons) My Favorite Things *Fibers:* (natural twine) May Arts *Template:* (debossing woodgrain) Papertrey Ink *Dies:* (labels) Papertrey Ink

## ⟨5⟩ Yellow Roses Love Card

**Designer: Nicky Hsu**

❶ Make card from cardstock; stamp sentiment.

❷ Stamp Rose Background on cardstock; overstamp Flourish Background. Color with markers and accent with glitter pen. Cut out and adhere, using foam tape as desired.

❸ Adhere pearls and tie on twill.

*Finished size: 4¼" x 5½"*

## ⟨5⟩ Delicate Thinking of You Card

**Designer: Janette Olen**

❶ Make card from cardstock.

❷ Mat patterned paper with cardstock panel. Stitch edges.

❸ Adhere ribbon and lace. Adhere panel to card.

❹ Stamp rose and sentiment on cardstock; color. Ink and stitch edges. Double-mat with cardstock and adhere with foam tape.

❺ Adhere pearls.

*Finished size: 4¼" x 5½"*

**SUPPLIES:** *Rubber stamps:* (Rose Background, Flourish Background) Hero Arts *Clear stamp:* (sentiment from Treasure the Moments set) Hero Arts *Dye ink:* (Rich Cocoa) Tsukineko; (Wild Honey) Ranger Industries *Cardstock:* (Rustic White, white) Papertrey Ink *Color media:* (cream, yellow, orange, green markers) Copic; (clear glitter pen) Sakura *Accents:* (white pearls) Michaels *Fibers:* (yellow twill) Papertrey Ink

**SUPPLIES:** *Clear stamps:* (rose from June Rose set; sentiment from Poppies & Greetings set) Sweet 'n Sassy Stamps *Dye ink:* (Tuxedo Black) Tsukineko *Specialty ink:* (Melon Berry hybrid) Papertrey Ink *Cardstock:* (Melon Berry) Papertrey Ink; (White Pearl Linen shimmer) PaperTemptress; (white) Neenah Paper *Patterned paper:* (peach floral from Home pad) My Mind's Eye *Color medium:* (assorted markers) Copic *Accents:* (white pearls) Michaels *Fibers:* (peach ribbon) Papertrey Ink; (white lace) Jo-Ann Stores

## :5: Turtle Valentine Card

**Designer: Wendy Ramlakhan**

1. Make card from cardstock.
2. Punch bottom edge of patterned paper. Tie on ribbon and adhere to card.
3. Stamp Special Delivery on cardstock panel. Trim, color, and paint. Mat with cardstock and adhere with foam tape.
4. Apply glitter glue to patterned paper.

*Finished size: 5" x 4¼"*

## Fashion Friend Gift Card Holder

**Designer: Wendy Ramlakhan**

1. Make card holder box. Die-cut large labels from patterned paper; adhere to front and back of card holder.
2. Die-cut small label from patterned paper; adhere.
3. Die-cut large oval from cardstock.
4. Stamp Shopping Willow on cardstock. Color, cut out, and adhere to oval.
5. Stamp Shopping Willow on patterned paper; cut out bags and adhere.
6. Adhere piece to card with foam tape; paint.
7. Print sentiment on cardstock; die-cut into small oval. Adhere with foam tape.

*Finished size: 3½" x 4¾"*

**SUPPLIES:** *Rubber stamp:* (Special Delivery) Karen's Doodles *Dye ink:* (Tuxedo Black) Tsukineko *Cardstock:* (Pinkini) Bazzill Basics Paper; (white) Papertrey Ink *Patterned paper:* (Blush Dot from Double Dot collection) BoBunny Press *Color medium:* (assorted markers) Copic *Paint:* (Pixie Dust) Shimmering Products *Accent:* (iridescent glitter glue) Ranger Industries *Fibers:* (pink ribbon) Offray *Tool:* (border punch) Martha Stewart Crafts

**SUPPLIES:** *Rubber stamp:* (Shopping Willow) Whiff of Joy *Dye ink:* (Tuxedo Black) Tsukineko *Cardstock:* (Vintage Cream) Papertrey Ink; (white) *Patterned paper:* (tiny floral, blue flowers, aqua, kraft from The Linen Closet pad) DCWV Inc. *Color medium:* (assorted markers) Copic *Paint:* (Pixie Dust) Shimmering Products *Fibers:* (brown ribbon) American Crafts *Font:* (Garton) www.fontspace.com *Dies:* (small, large labels; ovals) Spellbinders

DESIGNER TIPS

When airbrushing, use small, light bursts. You can always add more color, but you cannot take it away.

Use only the edge of the die to create a border.

To decide where to color highlights and shadows, see where the sunlight hits the image.

DESIGNER TIP

Color buttons to make them match the card.

## Just a Note Card

**Designer:** Kimberly Crawford

① Make card from cardstock.

② Die-cut and emboss scalloped square from cardstock; trim and adhere.

③ Stamp flowers on cardstock. Die-cut and emboss into rectangle. Color, airbrush, and adhere.

④ Stamp sentiment on cardstock. Die-cut and emboss into label; adhere with foam tape.

*Finished size: 4¼" x 5½"*

## Season's Greetings Card

**Designer:** Belinda Chang Langner

① Make card from cardstock; cover with cardstock.

② Stamp musical notes and nutcracker on cardstock; color. Die-cut into label and ink edges.

③ Cut patterned paper panel, adhere stamped label, and tie on ribbon. Adhere to card.

④ Stamp season's greetings on cardstock strip. Round corners, ink edges, and adhere.

⑤ Thread buttons with twine; adhere. Adhere rhinestone.

*Finished size: 4¼" x 5½"*

**SUPPLIES:** *Clear stamps:* (flowers from Delicate Blossoms set; sentiment from Everyday Sayings set) Hero Arts *Dye ink:* (Tuxedo Black) Tsukineko *Cardstock:* (Terra Cotta, Simply Chartreuse) Papertrey Ink; (white) Neenah Paper *Color medium:* (assorted markers) Copic *Dies:* (label, rectangle, scalloped square) Spellbinders *Tool:* (airbrush system) Copic

**SUPPLIES:** *Clear stamps:* (nutcracker, sentiment from Nutcracker Sweet set; musical notes from Musical Backgrounds set) Waltzingmouse Stamps *Dye ink:* (Chai, Chamomile) Papertrey Ink *Specialty ink:* (Ripe Avocado, Dark Chocolate hybrid) Papertrey Ink *Cardstock:* (Ripe Avocado, Vintage Cream) Papertrey Ink *Patterned paper:* (green grid from 2008 Bitty Box Basics collection) Papertrey Ink *Color medium:* (assorted markers) Copic *Accents:* (yellow buttons) Making Memories; (red rhinestone) Hero Arts *Fibers:* (red ribbon) Papertrey Ink; (natural twine) May Arts *Die:* (label) Spellbinders *Tool:* (corner rounder punch) We R Memory Keepers

Stamp veggies on die cut cardstock.

Stamp veggies on patterned paper.

Trim veggies from patterned paper and adhere to cardstock.

## 5 Steps Let's Get Together Card

**Designer: Kim Kesti**

1. Make card from cardstock; adhere cardstock rectangle.
2. Stamp sentiment on cardstock rectangle, stitch edges, and mat with patterned paper. Tie on fabric and adhere.
3. Die-cut scalloped oval from cardstock. Create stamped element, following figures 1–3.
4. Ink edges of piece and adhere to card with foam tape.

*Finished size: 4¼" x 6"*

**SUPPLIES:** *Clear stamps:* (veggies, sentiment from Kiss the Cook set) Hero Arts *Dye ink:* (Forest Foliage) Stampin' Up!; (Scattered Straw) Ranger Industries *Cardstock:* (Natural, Parakeet, Kisses, Tangelo Blast) Bazzill Basics Paper *Patterned paper:* (Sunshine from Garden Variety collection, Tailor Made from Material Girl collection) Cosmo Cricket; (Free from Unwritten collection) Reminisce; (Vine Dot from Just Chillin Girl collection) Making Memories *Die:* (scalloped oval) QuicKutz *Other:* (red gingham fabric) Jo-Ann Stores

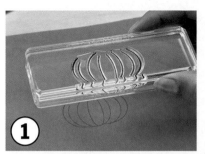

**1** Stamp pumpkin and flowers on patterned paper.

**2** Trim images, layer, and adhere to card. *Note: Adhere some pieces with foam tape.*

**3** Adhere sprinkles to centers of flowers.

## 5 STEPS Give Thanks Card

**Designer:** Heidi Van Laar

**①** Make card from cardstock; die-cut into label. *Note: Be careful not to cut across the fold.*

**②** Die-cut labels from patterned paper, adhere together, and tie on ribbon bow. Adhere to card.

**③** Die-cut circles from patterned paper. Stamp give and thanks on cardstock, trim, bend, and adhere between circles. Adhere piece to card with foam tape.

**④** Create stamped element, following figures 1–3. Adhere to card with foam tape.

*Finished size: 4" x 5½"*

---

DESIGNER TIP

Use low profile foam tape when adding multiple layers to your card. This will ensure that your card isn't too bulky for an envelope.

---

**SUPPLIES:** *Clear stamps:* (pumpkin, flowers, give, thanks from Happy Harvest set) i {heart} papers *Chalk ink:* (Chestnut Roan, Yellow Ochre) Clearsnap *Cardstock:* (white) Georgia-Pacific *Patterned paper:* (Sunny Brocade, Petit Floral, Linen, Dress Shirt from Lydia collection; Ice Cubes from Smoothie Shoppe collection) GCD Studios *Accent:* (multicolored sprinkles) Flower Soft *Fibers:* (blue ribbon) May Arts *Dies:* (circles, labels) Spellbinders

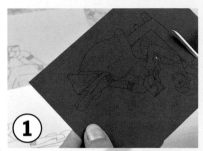

Print Reading Rachel stamp on cardstock and patterned paper.

Trim images; adhere. *Note: Do not trim image printed on Vintage Cream cardstock.*

Color image with pencils.

## For You Gift Card Holder

**Designer: Emily Branch**

1. Trim two cardstock rectangles. Adhere three sides to create pocket. Circle-punch right side.
2. Ink edges of envelope; adhere. Affix alphabet stickers and apply rub-on to library card to spell sentiment. Insert in envelope.
3. Create stamped element, following figures 1–3. Trim piece and round one corner.
4. Adhere patterned paper strips. Border-punch strip.
5. Trim circles from border sticker; affix. Tie on twine.
6. Adhere panel to card.

*Finished size: 6" x 4"*

**SUPPLIES:** *Pigment ink:* (Frost White) Clearsnap  *Chalk ink:* (Creamy Brown) Clearsnap  *Cardstock:* (Green Tea, brown) Bazzill Basics Paper; (Vintage Cream) Papertrey Ink  *Patterned paper:* (Affection, Free Spirit, Mellow, Headphones from Indie Girl collection) Sassafras Lass  *Color medium:* (dark brown, light brown, peach, pink pencils) Prismacolor  *Accents:* (kraft library card, envelope) Maya Road  *Digital element:* (Reading Rachel stamp) www.buysassystudiodesigns.blogspot.com  *Rub-on:* (you) Creative Imaginations  *Stickers:* (Tiny Type alphabet) Cosmo Cricket; (border) Sassafras Lass  *Fibers:* (natural jute twine) May Arts  *Tools:* (circle, corner rounder punches) Stampin' Up!; (border punch) EK Success

Stamp butterfly on card; color with marker.

Stamp butterfly on patterned paper; trim.

Accent with gel pen and adhere trimmed pieces to card. *Note: Adhere top piece with foam tape.*

## Butterfly Hello Card

Designer: Vanessa Menhorn

1 Make card from cardstock.

2 Create stamped element, following figures 1–3.

3 Stamp flower on card. Stamp flower on patterned paper, color flower center with marker, and trim. Adhere pieces to card.

4 Adhere patterned paper strips. *Note: Border-punch one strip before adhering.*

5 Stamp hello friend and round right corners.

*Finished size: 4¼" x 5½"*

**SUPPLIES:** *Rubber stamp:* (butterfly from Butterflies set) Hero Arts *Clear stamps:* (flower from Be Happy set, sentiment from Love That set) Hero Arts *Dye ink:* (Basic Black) Stampin' Up! *Cardstock:* (kraft) Papertrey Ink *Patterned paper:* (Saltwater Taffy, Tee Time, Pink Fizz, Frosted Berry from Lemonade collection; Lexicon from Basics collection) BasicGrey *Color media:* (yellow, brown markers) Copic; (white gel pen) American Crafts *Tools:* (border punch) Fiskars; (corner rounder punch)

DESIGNER TIP

It's helpful to have a tiny pair of sharp scissors on hand for trimming stamped images with lots of detail.

DESIGNER TIP

Paper piecing is a great way to use up your patterned paper scraps.

## 5 STEPS Live in the Moment Card

Designer: Emily Niehaus

① Make card from cardstock, round bottom corners, and ink edges.

② Stamp dress on cardstock and patterned paper. Trim pieces and adhere. Adhere rhinestone.

③ Border-punch cardstock; adhere.

④ Adhere ribbon around front flap. Tie on string and adhere button.

⑤ Stamp sentiment on cardstock, punch into circle, and adhere.

*Finished size: 4¼" x 5½"*

## 5 STEPS Enjoy the Journey Card

Designer: Amy Wanford

① Make card from cardstock; round top corners.

② Stamp shadow. Stamp bicycle on card, cardstock, and patterned paper. Trim cardstock and patterned paper; adhere.

③ Stamp sentiment and draw lines with pen.

*Finished size: 4¼" square*

**SUPPLIES:** *Clear stamps:* (dress from Dresses with Sashes set) Crescendoh; (sentiment from Life Lines set) Flourishes *Dye ink:* (Tuxedo Black) Tsukineko; (Old Paper) Ranger Industries *Cardstock:* (Crumb Cake, Very Vanilla) Stampin' Up! *Patterned paper:* (One of a Kind from The Thrift Shop collection) October Afternoon *Accents:* (cream rhinestone button) Jenni Bowlin Studio; (red rhinestone) *Fibers:* (black ribbon) Offray; (cream string) *Tools:* (circle punch) Stampin' Up!; (border punch) Martha Stewart Crafts; (corner rounder punch)

**SUPPLIES:** *Clear stamps:* (bicycle, sentiment, shadow from The Whole Cycle set) Practicing Creativity Designs *Dye ink:* (Tuxedo Black) Tsukineko *Watermark ink:* Tsukineko *Cardstock:* (Smokey Shadow, kraft) Papertrey Ink *Patterned paper:* (yellow grid from 2008 Bitty Box Basics collection, red polka dot from 2008 Bitty Dot Basics collection) Papertrey Ink *Color medium:* (black pen) *Tool:* (corner rounder punch) We R Memory Keepers

DESIGNER TIP
Don't limit your stamping surface to paper. Fabric is fun to stamp and comes in a wide variety of patterns.

## Happy Life Card
Designer: Kelley Eubanks

1. Make card from cardstock; round bottom corners.
2. Stamp Gown on card and on cardstock. Trim cardstock; adhere. Apply glitter glue.
3. Stamp sentiment, adhere rhinestone, and tie on ribbon bow.

*Finished size: 4½" square*

## Let's Get Together Card
Designer: Laurel Seabrook

1. Make card from cardstock; adhere fabric.
2. Stamp shadow and picture on cardstock strip. Color with markers and adhere. Stitch border and zigzag-stitch seams.
3. Stamp couch on fabric and cardstock, trim, and adhere. *Note: Adhere couch cushions with foam tape.*
4. Stamp sentiment on cardstock strip; adhere with foam tape.

*Finished size: 4" square*

**SUPPLIES:** *Rubber stamp:* (Gown) A Muse Artstamps *Clear stamp:* (sentiment from Wishing You...set) Papertrey Ink *Dye ink:* (Tuxedo Black) Tsukineko *Cardstock:* (Smoky, Cashmere) Bazzill Basics Paper; (white) Papertrey Ink *Accents:* (clear rhinestone) Kaisercraft; (iridescent glitter glue) Ranger Industries *Fibers:* (black ribbon) Offray *Tools:* (corner rounder punch) Stampin' Up!

**SUPPLIES:** *Clear stamps:* (couch, picture, sentiment from On My Couch set; shadow from On My Couch Additions set) Papertrey Ink *Dye ink:* (Grey Wool, black) Close To My Heart *Cardstock:* (white, brown) Close To My Heart *Color medium:* (black, gray, yellow markers) Copic *Other:* (gray floral, yellow floral fabric)

## Right at Home Card

Designer: Alanna Harris

1. Make card from patterned paper; adhere patterned paper strip.

2. Stamp lamps on cardstock rectangle and patterned paper. Trim patterned paper and adhere.

3. Adhere pearls and pierce lines. Mat with cardstock and adhere to card with foam tape.

4. Die-cut label from cardstock, stamp sentiment, and adhere to card with foam tape.

*Finished size: 5½" x 4¼"*

## Call Me Anytime Card

Designer: AJ Otto

1. Make card from cardstock; adhere strip from phone book page.

2. Adhere ribbon around front flap and tie with string.

3. Die-cut circle from cardstock and label from cork. Adhere circle to card with foam tape.

4. Stamp phone and sentiment on cork label and phone book page. Trim phone book page and adhere. Adhere piece to card.

5. Thread buttons with string and adhere to card.

*Finished size: 4¼" x 5½"*

**SUPPLIES:** *Rubber stamp:* (Lamp) A Muse Artstamps *Clear stamp:* (sentiment from Boards & Beams set) Papertrey Ink *Specialty ink:* (Noir hybrid) Tsukineko *Cardstock:* (Basic Black) Stampin' Up!; (white) Gina K Designs *Patterned paper:* (Petite Gingham Black) A Muse Artstamps; (Peculiar, Nonchalant, Light Hearted from Offbeat collection) BasicGrey *Accents:* (red pearls) A Muse Artstamps *Die:* (label) Ellison

**SUPPLIES:** *Rubber stamps:* (phone, sentiment from Everyday Adorable set) Unity Stamp Co. *Dye ink:* (Tuxedo Black) Tsukineko *Cardstock:* (Crumb Cake, Basic Black) Stampin' Up! *Accents:* (red buttons) *Fibers:* (red stitched ribbon) Papertrey Ink; (white string) *Dies:* (circle, label) Spellbinders *Other:* (cork, phone book page)

DESIGNER TIP

Fill this box with candy or jewelry for a fun birthday or thank you gift for your friend.

## Hello Friend Box

Designer: Michele Hetland

1. Die-cut scalloped circles from cardstock; pierce holes in one circle. Trim 1½" wide cardstock strip.

2. Stamp triple circle, hello, and friend on pierced circle. Stamp large flower and leaves on patterned paper, trim, and adhere to pierced circle. *Note: Adhere center of flower with foam tape.*

3. Stamp vine and leaves on cardstock strip. Stamp small flowers on patterned paper, trim, and adhere to strip.

4. Adhere strip to scalloped circle to create box lid.

5. Cut second cardstock strip 1½" wide. Adhere to scalloped circle to create box base.

6. Let pieces dry overnight and then carefully slide one over the other to create box.

*Finished size: 3½" diameter x 1½" height*

## Thanks{give}ing Card

Designer: Ashley Harris

1. Make card from cardstock; stamp Pumpkin.

2. Stamp Pumpkin on patterned paper, trim, and adhere.

3. Apply rub-on.

*Finished size: 4" square*

**SUPPLIES:** *Clear stamps:* (flowers, vine, leaf, hello, friend from Flower Garden set; triple circle from Borders & Corners {circle} set) Papertrey Ink *Chalk ink:* (Lime Pastel) Clearsnap *Specialty ink:* (Dark Chocolate hybrid) Papertrey Ink *Cardstock:* (Rustic Cream) Papertrey Ink *Patterned paper:* (red, yellow polka dots from 2008 Bitty Dot Basics collection) Papertrey Ink; (Tree Tops from A Walk in the Park collection) Echo Park Paper *Die:* (scalloped circle) Spellbinders

**SUPPLIES:** *Clear stamp:* (Pumpkin) Imaginisce *Dye ink:* (black) Stewart Superior Corp. *Cardstock:* (Cream Puff) Bazzill Basics Paper *Patterned paper:* (Changing Leaves, Cinnamon Sticks, Autumn Splendor from Apple Cider collection) Imaginisce *Rub-on:* (thanks{give}ing) Imaginisce

## ⑤ Birthday Banner Card

Designer: Teri Anderson

❶ Make card from cardstock; stamp happy birthday.

❷ Stamp pennants and flowers on cardstock. Trim and adhere to card.

❸ Draw lines with marker to connect pennants. Adhere rhinestone.

*Finished size: 3¾" square*

## ⑤ Color My World Card

Designer: Betsy Veldman

❶ Make card from cardstock.

❷ Punch circles from patterned paper; adhere to patterned paper rectangle.

❸ Stitch panel, ink edges, and tie on string. Adhere to card.

❹ Stamp oval frame on cardstock. Punch into scalloped oval and ink edges. Stamp sentiment on oval and patterned paper. Trim and adhere. *Note: Adhere some letters with foam tape.*

❺ Adhere piece to card with foam tape.

*Finished size: 3¾" x 5¾"*

**SUPPLIES:** *Clear stamps:* (pennant from Bannerific set; happy birthday, flower from Sophie's Sentiments set) Lawn Fawn *Solvent ink:* (Jet Black) Tsukineko *Cardstock:* (red, orange, yellow, green, blue) Bazzill Basics Paper; (white) Georgia-Pacific *Color medium:* (black marker) *Accent:* (red rhinestone) Kaisercraft

**SUPPLIES:** *Clear stamps:* (oval frame from Borders & Corners {oval} set) Papertrey Ink; (sentiment from Priceless Love Word Puzzle set) Close To My Heart *Chalk ink:* (Creamy Brown) Clearsnap *Pigment ink:* (Spring Rain) Papertrey Ink *Specialty ink:* (True Black hybrid) Papertrey Ink *Cardstock:* (Spring Rain, Vintage Cream) Papertrey Ink *Patterned paper:* (Deck the Hollies from Mitten Weather collection) Cosmo Cricket; (Shabby Flower, Vintage Patchwork from Paper Girl collection) The Girls' Paperie; (Vacancy/Blue Weave from Pack Your Bags collection) Little Yellow Bicycle; (Favorite Thing Colorful Umbrellas from Quite Contrary collection) My Mind's Eye *Fibers:* (red/white, blue/white string) Papertrey Ink *Tools:* (scalloped oval punch) Marvy Uchida; (circle punches) EK Success

**DESIGNER TIP**
Use the sections you cut from your tree to make more tags! You'll have a forest of tree tags in no time at all.

**DESIGNER TIP**
Try bending clear sentiment stamps for a custom look.

## Joy Tag

Designer: Sarah Windisch

1. Die-cut tag from cardstock; adhere patterned paper strip.

2. Stamp sentiment; color with pencil and pen.

3. Stamp tree on patterned paper, trim, and adhere together. Punch star from cardstock; adhere. Accent piece with marker.

4. Adhere piece to tag with foam tape. Punch holes and tie on ribbon.

*Finished size: 2¼" x 3¾"*

## Birthday Monster Box

Designer: Chan Vuong

1. Deboss cardstock square; adhere to box.

2. Affix stickers. Stamp cityscape and happy birthday on cardstock, trim, and adhere with foam tape.

3. Stamp flames on patterned paper, trim, and adhere with foam tape.

4. Stamp monster on cardstock and patterned paper. Trim, adhere, color belly with marker, and adhere to box with foam tape.

*Finished size: 3½" x 3½" x 1"*

**SUPPLIES:** *Clear stamps:* (tree from Kelly Panacci Christmas set) Sandylion; (sentiment from Joy Christmas set) Studio G *Solvent ink:* (Jet Black) Tsukineko *Cardstock:* (Manila) Roselle Paper Co.; (Marigold glitter) DCWV Inc. *Patterned paper:* (Snow Cap, Alpine, Evergreen, Frost, Snow Globe, Village from Eskimos Kisses collection) BasicGrey *Color media:* (blue pencil, pink glitter pen, black marker) *Fibers:* (tan ribbon) Offray *Die:* (tag) QuicKutz *Tool:* (star punch) Marvy Uchida

**SUPPLIES:** *Clear stamps:* (monster, flames, cityscape from Eeek! A Monster! set) My Cute Stamps; (happy birthday from Sophie's Sentiments set) Lawn Fawn *Pigment ink:* (Onyx Black) Tsukineko *Cardstock:* (Plum Pudding, Vintage Cream) Papertrey Ink *Patterned paper:* (Preserve from Sweet Marmalade collection) Sassafras Lass; (orange stars from Matilda pad) Cosmo Cricket *Color medium:* (teal marker) Copic *Stickers:* (black glitter stars) American Crafts *Template:* (debossing canvas) Papertrey Ink *Other:* (kraft gift box)

**①** Stamp dog on cardstock. Stamp dog on repositionable note; trim to create mask.

**②** Adhere mask over stamped dog.

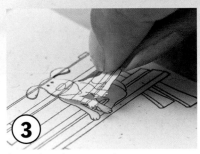

**③** Stamp bench over mask. Remove mask dog.

## :5: Just Sittin' Here Card

**Designer: Kim Hughes**

❶ Make card from cardstock.

❷ Adhere patterned paper strip to cardstock rectangle, stitch edges, and adhere to card.

❸ Create stamped element, following figures 1–3.

❹ Remove mask and stamp sentiment.

❺ Border-punch panel, tie on string, and adhere to card.

*Finished size: 4¾" x 4¼"*

---

DESIGNER TIP

Use precision scissors or a craft knife to cut your stamped image.

---

**SUPPLIES:** *Rubber stamps:* (bench, dog, sentiment from In the Park set) Taylored Expressions *Dye ink:* (Early Espresso) Stampin' Up! *Cardstock:* (Vintage Vines Ruby Slipper embossed, Sugar Cream) Bazzill Basics Paper; (Rustic White) Papertrey Ink *Patterned paper:* (Best of Friends Share from Quite Contrary collection) My Mind's Eye *Fibers:* (green/white string) Papertrey Ink *Tool:* (border punch) EK Success *Other:* (repositionable note) 3M

**1** Adhere die cut borders to cardstock with repositionable adhesive. Spritz shimmer sprays over masks.

**2** Remove masks; stamp dotted tickets and calendars.

**3** Stamp stars.

## All-Star Birthday Card
Designer: Betsy Veldman

*Ink all edges*

1. Make card from cardstock; die-cut ticket borders from cardstock.
2. Create stamped element, following figures 1–3.
3. Die-cut label from patterned paper, trim, and adhere to stamped panel with foam tape.
4. Die-cut ticket border from cardstock, trim, and spritz with shimmer sprays.
5. Stamp dotted ticket, happy birthday, and star oval on piece. Sew on buttons with string. Adhere piece with foam tape and tie string around panel.
6. Adhere panel to card and stitch borders.

*Finished size: 4¼" x 5½"*

**SUPPLIES:** *Clear stamps:* (dotted ticket, calendar, happy birthday, star oval from Just the Ticket set; star from All-Star Team set) Papertrey Ink *Dye ink:* (Tea Dye) Ranger Industries; (Real Red) Stampin' Up! *Pigment ink:* (Aqua Mist) Papertrey Ink *Chalk ink:* (Chestnut Roan) Clearsnap *Specialty ink:* (Scarlet, Mimosa shimmer spray) Tattered Angels *Cardstock:* (Vintage Cream, Aqua Mist, black) Papertrey Ink *Patterned paper:* (General Store from Curio collection) BasicGrey *Accents:* (teal buttons) Papertrey Ink *Fibers:* (red/white string) Papertrey Ink *Adhesive:* (repositionable) *Dies:* (ticket border, label) Papertrey Ink

### DESIGNER TIP

Use stamps that have coordinating die cuts. This makes creating your masks quick and easy and ensures a perfect match every time!

**1** Trim strip from cardstock. Place negative over card and stamp holly leaf repeatedly.

**2** Remove mask and reposition on card. Stamp holly leaf repeatedly.

**3** Continue masking and stamping until card is covered. Accent berries with glitter glue.

## 5 STEPS Deck the Halls Card

**Designer:** Cristina Kowalczyk

1. Make card from cardstock; ink edges.
2. Create stamped element, following figures 1–3.
3. Stamp sentiment and accent with glitter glue.

*Finished size: 4¼" x 5½"*

**SUPPLIES:** *Clear stamps:* (holly leaf from Holiday Gift Tags set) Hero Arts; (sentiment) *Dye ink:* (Peeled Paint) Ranger Industries *Pigment ink:* (Vintage Sepia) Tsukineko *Cardstock:* (Vintage Cream, white) Papertrey Ink *Accent:* (red glitter glue) Ranger Industries

DESIGNER TIP

For best results, gently pounce Angel Pink ink over mask with a sponge. This will keep your card soft and delicate all while giving you more control.

DESIGNER TIP

Masking is all about precision so make sure you clean your stamps thoroughly after each impression.

DESIGNER TIP

For best results, gently pounce Angel Pink ink over mask with a sponge. This will keep your card soft and delicate all while giving you more control.

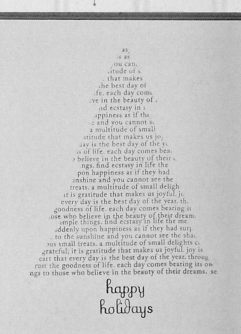

## Happy Holidays Card
**Designer:** Cristina Kowalczyk

1. Make card from cardstock.

2. Adhere repositionable notes, at an angle, directly to stamp. Ink stamp, remove notes, and stamp on cardstock rectangle. Clean stamp and repeat down cardstock to create tree.

3. Adhere repositionable note to holidays portion of Happy Holidays stamp. Ink happy; remove note and stamp. Clean stamp and repeat with holidays.

4. Mat panel with cardstock and adhere to card.

*Finished size: 4¼" x 5¼"*

## To Mom Card
**Designer:** Julie Masse

1. Make card from cardstock.

2. Stamp lily silhouette, high light, and low light on cardstock rectangle.

3. Mask lily with cardstock and repositionable adhesive. Die-cut oval from cardstock. Place negative over cardstock, and ink.

4. Remove masks and stamp to, mom. Round top corners and adhere to patterned paper panel.

5. Die-cut border from cardstock strip; adhere. Adhere pearls and tie on ribbon.

6. Adhere panel to card.

*Finished size: 4" x 6"*

**SUPPLIES:** *Rubber stamp:* (Happy Holidays) Impress Rubber Stamps *Clear stamp:* (typewriter text from Background Basics: Text Style set) Papertrey Ink *Dye ink:* (Cottage Ivy, Rich Cocoa) Tsukineko *Cardstock:* (New Leaf, kraft, white) Papertrey Ink *Other:* (repositionable notes) 3M

**SUPPLIES:** *Clear stamps:* (lily silhouette, high light, low light from A Year of Thanks II with Multi Step Lily of the Valley set; to, mom from Whole Family set) Kitchen Sink Stamps *Dye ink:* (Angel Pink, Bamboo Leaves, New Sprout) Tsukineko *Specialty ink:* (New Leaf hybrid) Papertrey Ink *Cardstock:* (Soft Stone, Sweet Blush) Papertrey Ink; (white) Gina K Designs *Patterned paper:* (pink damask from Pretty Pastels collection) Papertrey Ink *Accents:* (pink pearls) Kaisercraft *Fibers:* (pink polka dot ribbon) Papertrey Ink *Adhesive:* (repositionable) *Dies:* (oval) Spellbinders; (scalloped border) Papertrey Ink *Tool:* (corner rounder punch) Creative Memories

DESIGNER TIP
Look to common office supplies such as tags, envelopes, twine, and tickets for a little unexpected inspiration.

DESIGNER TIP
Masking with repositionable notes is faster than using repositionable adhesive and a great way to create basic masked shapes in no time at all.

## 5 STEPS Smile Tag
**Designer: Michelle Mathey**

1. Lay chipboard leaves on tag; spritz with shimmer spray. Let dry.
2. Remove chipboard masks; stamp sentiment and Wrought Scroll.
3. Fray burlap and attach to tag with staples. Tie on ribbon, thread button with ribbon, and adhere.
4. Tie ribbon to top of tag and tie on twine.

*Finished size: 2½" x 5"*

## 5 STEPS Ahoy Card
**Designer: Cristina Kowalczyk**

1. Make card from cardstock.
2. Trim repositionable notes into square and rectangle; adhere. Stamp offset scallops.
3. Remove masks.
4. Stamp frame, boat, and "Ahoy".

*Finished size: 4" x 5½"*

**SUPPLIES:** *Rubber stamp:* (Wrought Scroll) Stampington & Co. *Clear stamp:* (sentiment from Signature Greetings set) Papertrey Ink *Dye ink:* (Tuxedo Black) Tsukineko *Chalk ink:* (Creamy Brown) Clearsnap *Specialty ink:* (Key Lime Pie shimmer spray) Tattered Angels *Accents:* (chipboard leaves) Cosmo Cricket; (manila tag) Office Depot; (silver staples, cream button) *Fibers:* (white ribbon, natural twine) Papertrey Ink *Other:* (burlap) Hobby Lobby

**SUPPLIES:** *Rubber stamp:* (2¼ Inch Frame) Impress Rubber Stamps *Clear stamps:* (boat from Baby Boy set) Inkadinkado; (Fresh Alphabet; offset scallops from Background Basics: Retro set) Papertrey Ink *Dye ink:* (Tangelo, Bahama Blue, Danube Blue) Tsukineko *Pigment ink:* (Sky Blue) Inkadinkado *Chalk ink:* (Turquoise) Inkadinkado *Cardstock:* (white) Papertrey Ink *Other:* (repositionable note) 3M

DESIGNER TIP
Keep it clean! Use a paper towel to remove excess mist from sticker masks.

## ABC Tag

**Designer: Lori Tecler**

1. Stamp apple on cardstock rectangle.

2. Mask apple with cardstock and repositionable adhesive. Stamp books.

3. Mask books with cardstock and repositionable adhesive. Stamp alphabet.

4. Remove masks, color images with markers, and adhere to cardstock.

5. Adhere panel to tag. Trim bottom of tag and tie on ribbon.

*Finished size: 2½" x 4"*

## Birthday Numbers Card

**Designer: Teri Anderson**

1. Make card from cardstock.

2. Affix numbers to cardstock rectangle; spritz with shimmer spray. Let dry and remove stickers. Adhere panel to card.

3. Stamp Cupcake on cardstock, color with markers, and trim. Adhere to card.

4. Stamp happy birthday on cardstock strip, adhere rhinestones, and adhere to card.

*Designs  Finished size: 4¼" x 6½"*

**SUPPLIES:** *Clear stamps:* (alphabet, books, apple from ABC123 set) Clear & Simple Stamps *Dye ink:* (London Fog) Tsukineko *Specialty ink:* (Perfect Little Black Dress) Clear & Simple Stamps *Cardstock:* (A Blanc Check, Dare to Be a Diva Red) Clear & Simple Stamps *Color medium:* (brown, red, green markers) Copic *Accent:* (manila tag) Staples *Fibers:* (red ribbon) Michaels *Adhesive:* (repositionable)

**SUPPLIES:** *Rubber stamp:* (Cupcake) Studio G  *Clear stamp:* (happy birthday from Sophie's Sentiments set) Lawn Fawn *Dye ink:* (Jet Black) Tsukineko *Specialty ink:* (Yellow Daisy shimmer spray) Tattered Angels *Cardstock:* (white) Georgia-Pacific *Color medium:* (red, blue, yellow markers) Copic *Accents:* (red rhinestones) Kaisercraft *Stickers:* (numbers) Heidi Grace Designs

DESIGNER TIP
Place a mouse pad inside your gift bag before stamping. This will help keep your impressions even.

## Father's Day Gift Bag

**Designer:** Jaclyn Miller

1. Stamp bird on gift bag.
2. Mask bird with cardstock and repositionable adhesive. Stamp scripted text and remove mask.
3. Stamp sentiment and tie on ribbon.

*Finished size: 4½" x 5½"*

## Happy Harvest Candle

**Designer:** Julie Campbell

1. Die-cut rickrack borders from felt; adhere to candle. Adhere patterned paper strip and twine.
2. Die-cut label from cardstock. Stamp round pumpkins.
3. Mask round pumpkins with cardstock and repositionable adhesive. Stamp plaid basket and pumpkins.
4. Remove mask, stamp happy harvest, color images, and ink edges. Adhere to candle with foam tape.
5. Thread button with twine and adhere.

*Finished size: 2¾" diameter x 4" height*

**SUPPLIES:** *Clear stamps:* (bird, scripted text from Artful Things set) Stamper Anonymous; (sentiment from Fillable Frames #4 set) Papertrey Ink *Dye ink:* (Chocolate, Sunflower, Autumn Terracotta) Close To My Heart *Cardstock:* (white) *Fibers:* (brown stitched ribbon) Bazzill Basics Paper *Adhesive:* (repositionable) *Other:* (kraft gift bag) Hobby Lobby

**SUPPLIES:** *Clear stamp:* (happy harvest, plaid basket, pumpkins, round pumpkins from Vintage Picnic set) Papertrey Ink *Dye ink:* (Tuxedo Black) Tsukineko; (Antique Linen) Ranger Industries *Chalk ink:* (Dark Brown) Clearsnap *Cardstock:* (Rustic Cream) Papertrey Ink *Patterned paper:* (Anything for You Helpful Houndstooth from So Sophie collection) My Mind's Eye *Color medium:* (assorted markers) Copic *Accent:* (brown button) My Favorite Things *Fibers:* (natural jute twine) May Arts *Adhesive:* (repositionable) *Dies:* (rickrack border, label) Papertrey Ink *Other:* (orange felt) Heather Bailey; (yellow candle)

DESIGNER TIP

Pounce your ink over the mask with a foam applicator to avoid smudging your image.

## Thank You Flower Card

**Designer: Sarah J. Moerman**

1. Make card from cardstock.
2. Adhere patterned paper rectangle and stitch edges.
3. Stamp Old Letter Writing on canvas; ink edges.
4. Die-cut flower from cardstock, place negative on fabric, and color with ink. Remove mask.
5. Tie twine around piece and affix to card.
6. Die-cut tag from cardstock, stamp thank you, and ink edges. Attach to twine with straight pin; adhere with foam tape.

*Finished size: 5½" x 4¼"*

## 5 STEPS Welcome Card

**Designer: Vanessa Menhorn**

1. Make card from cardstock.
2. Stamp sentiment and solid door on cardstock rectangle. Stamp outlined door.
3. Mask door with cardstock and repositionable adhesive. Stamp outlined doors and remove mask.
4. Double-mat panel with cardstock and adhere to card.

*Finished size: 4¼" x 5½"*

---

**SUPPLIES:** *Rubber stamp:* (Old Letter Writing) Hero Arts *Clear stamp:* (thank you from Classic Messages set) Hero Arts *Dye ink:* (Frayed Burlap, Barn Door, Peeled Paint, Shabby Shutters) Ranger Industries *Cardstock:* (kraft) Papertrey Ink *Patterned paper:* (Lexicon from Basics collection) BasicGrey *Accent:* (red flower stick pin) Making Memories *Fibers:* (white, natural jute twine) Papertrey Ink *Die:* (tag) Spellbinders; (flower) QuicKutz *Other:* (white adhesive-back canvas) Ranger Industries

**SUPPLIES:** *Clear stamps:* (solid door, outlined door, sentiment from Home Made set) Papertrey Ink *Dye ink:* (Tuxedo Black) Tsukineko *Pigment ink:* (Satin Red) Tsukineko *Cardstock:* (Pure Poppy, black, white) Papertrey Ink *Adhesive:* (repositionable)

**1** Spritz specialty paper with shimmer sprays.

**2** Sprinkle salt; emboss.

**3** Remove salt; stamp flowers and dragonfly.

## Whole World Kin Card

**Designer: Teri Anderson**

1. Make card from cardstock; adhere patterned paper.
2. Create stamped element, following figures 1–3. Trim and adhere to card.
3. Stamp sentiment on cardstock strip, tie on twine, and adhere.
4. Adhere rhinestones.

*Finished size: 5½" x 4¼"*

---

DESIGNER TIP

Spritz with your lighter inks first and then layer on the darker shades.

---

**SUPPLIES:** *Clear stamps:* (flower, dragonfly, sentiment from Wildflowers set) Crafty Secrets *Solvent ink:* (Jet Black) Tsukineko *Specialty ink:* (Blue Skies, Yellow Daisy shimmer spray) Tattered Angels *Cardstock:* (Vintage Cream) Papertrey Ink; (white) Georgia-Pacific *Patterned paper:* (Ledger from Basics collection) BasicGrey *Specialty paper:* (glossy photo) *Accents:* (black rhinestones) Kaisercraft *Fibers:* (white jute twine) *Other:* (coarse salt)

Stamp rose on cardstock; emboss.
Mask rose and stamp leaves: emboss.

Spritz shimmer sprays on transparency
sheet. Paint rose using shimmer sprays
and paintbrush.

Repeat Step 2 to color leaves.

Happy Mother's Day

## 5 Rose for Mom Card

Designer: Maile Belles

1 Make card from cardstock.

2 Create stamped element, following figures 1–3.

3 Stamp sentiment on panel, trim, and tie on ribbon bow.

4 Adhere panel to card.

*Finished size: 7" x 3½"*

**DESIGNER TIPS**

See pgs. 168-170 for step-by-step
instructions for masking.

Shimmer sprays tend to settle to
the bottom of the bottle quickly so
make sure you shake them up before
spraying.

Paint the rose and leaves with the
lightest colors first and then go back
to add darker shadows.

**SUPPLIES:** *Clear stamps:* (rose, leaf from Year of Flowers: Roses set; sentiment from Delightful Dahlia set) Papertrey Ink *Pigment ink:* (Fresh Snow) Papertrey Ink *Specialty ink:* (Apple, Vintage Pink shimmer spray) Tattered Angels *Embossing powder:* (white) Jo-Ann Stores *Cardstock:* (Simply Chartreuse, white) Papertrey Ink *Transparency sheet; Fibers:* (white ribbon) Papertrey Ink

**1** Ink cardstock tag with dye ink; spritz with shimmer spray.

**2** Wet large clock stamp with water and stamp on tag. Repeat with large clock and number border.

**3** Dry tag with heat tool and spritz with shimmer spray.

## I Owe You Tag

**Designer: Valerie Mangan**

1 Cut cardstock into tag.

2 Create stamped element, following figures 1–3. Punch rounded rectangle.

3 Stamp sentiment on cardstock and adhere behind rounded rectangle.

4 Mat tag with patterned paper and stitch edges.

5 Stamp clock frame, clock numbers and hands on cardstock. Trim and adhere to tag. Adhere acetate clock.

6 Tie on string bow and attach safety pin. Punch hole and tie on ribbon.

*Finished size: 3¼" x 5¾"*

### DESIGNER TIPS

Stamping with water works best with Ranger Industries' Distress Ink because the ink remains "active" a few minutes after it's applied.

The more water you use and the harder you press into your inked surface, the more prominent your impression will be.

**SUPPLIES:** *Rubber stamp:* (sentiment from FYI set) Stampin' Up! *Clear stamps:* (clock frame, clock numbers, hands, number border, large clock from Make it Count set) Close To My Heart *Dye ink:* (black) Tsukineko; (Broken China) Ranger Industries *Specialty ink:* (Dazzling Diamonds shimmer spray) Tattered Angels *Cardstock:* (kraft) Bazzill Basics Paper; (Colonial White) Close To My Heart *Patterned paper:* (Fresh Air from Garden Gala collection) Webster's Pages *Accents:* (clear acetate clock) Heidi Swapp; (pewter safety pin) Tim Holtz *Fibers:* (brown/white string) Martha Stewart Crafts; (black ribbon) *Tool:* (rounded rectangle punch) Stampin' Up!

**DESIGNER TIPS**

Ink your sentiment stamps with markers in order to get two colors on one stamp.

The star stickers on this card are sticky on both sides which makes them perfect for adding sparkly glitter or fun flock.

**DESIGNER TIP**

Spritz more shimmer spray in the center of the cracked image to create a more dramatic focal point.

## Groovin' Guitar Card

**Designer: Carolyn King**

1. Make card from cardstock; spritz with shimmer spray.
2. Stamp sentiment and affix stickers. Adhere glitter.
3. Stamp guitar neck and flame body on cardstock, color with markers, and trim. Adhere to card with foam tape.
4. Adhere patterned paper strips and rhinestones.

*Finished size: 4¾" x 5"*

## You Rock! Card

**Designer: Kris Chirhart**

1. Make card from cardstock; adhere slightly smaller rectangle of sandpaper.
2. Spritz shimmer spray on inside front section of embossing folder. Emboss cardstock rectangle and let dry.
3. Attach brads to panel, double-mat with cardstock, and adhere.
4. Punch stars from cardstock and patterned paper; adhere with foam tape. Cut ring from cardstock using circle cutter; adhere.
5. Stamp Extreme Skateboard on cardstock; heat-emboss. Trim and adhere with foam tape.

*Finished size: 6¾" x 5½"*

**SUPPLIES:** *Rubber stamps:* (you rock, guitar neck, guitar flame body from You're My Hero set) Taylored Expressions *Dye ink:* (Tuxedo Black) Tsukineko *Specialty ink:* (Dewberry shimmer spray) Tattered Angels *Cardstock:* (white) Gina K Designs *Patterned paper:* (Party Line from Modern Homemaker collection) October Afternoon; (Horizon from Twilight collection) Pink Paislee *Color medium:* (yellow, orange, red markers) Copic *Accents:* (clear rhinestones) Kaisercraft; (yellow glitter) Doodlebug Design *Stickers:* (stars) *Tool:* (corner rounder punch) Creative Memories

**SUPPLIES:** *Rubber stamps:* (you rock! from Just Jawing set, Extreme Skateboard) Stampin' Up! *Watermark ink:* Tsukineko *Embossing powder:* (black) Stampin' Up! *Specialty ink:* (Spring Rain shimmer spray) Tattered Angels *Cardstock:* (Basic Black, Rich Razzleberry, Marina Mist) Stampin' Up!; (white) Georgia-Pacific *Patterned paper:* (polka dots from Razzleberry Lemonade collection) Stampin' Up! *Die:* (embossing Cracked) Ellison *Tools:* (extra large, large star punches) Stampin' Up!; (circle cutter) Creative Memories *Other:* (black sandpaper) 3M

**DESIGNER TIPS**

Achieve a light misting by spraying your surface from a distance.

Create a 3D effect by keeping your butterfly sticker on its original backing. Trim the sticker, fold it in half, and adhere the center with foam tape.

## :5: Miss You Card
**Designer: Maile Belles**

❶ Make card from cardstock.

❷ Spritz shimmer spray on transparency sheet. Ink Clouds stamp, and stamp on specialty paper. Trim and adhere to card.

❸ Stamp tree, Bird in Cage, and miss you.

❹ Trim leaves from cardstock; adhere. Tie ribbon bow; adhere.

*Finished size: 4" square*

## :5: True Friendship Tag
**Designer: Windy Robinson**

❶ Stamp flourishes on tag; emboss.

❷ Spritz tag with shimmer sprays. Let dry.

❸ Stamp sentiment and ink edges of tag.

❹ Adhere butterfly; tie on ribbon bow and twine.

*Finished size: 3" x 6¼"*

**SUPPLIES:** *Rubber stamps:* (Bird in Cage, Clouds) Hero Arts  *Clear stamps:* (tree from Falling Leaves set, miss you from Fillable Frames #7 set) Papertrey Ink  *Specialty ink:* (Noir hybrid) Stewart Superior Corp.; (Dark Chocolate, Ripe Avocado hybrid) Papertrey Ink; (Sky Blue shimmer spray) Tattered Angels  *Cardstock:* (Simply Chartreuse, white) Papertrey Ink; (Hillary) Bazzill Basics Paper  *Specialty paper:* (watercolor)  *Transparency sheet; Fibers:* (white ribbon) Papertrey Ink

**SUPPLIES:** *Rubber stamps:* (sentiment, flourish from Tattered Elements set) Stampers Anonymous  *Dye ink:* (Shabby Shutters, Walnut Stain) Ranger Industries  *Specialty ink:* (Burnt Umber hybrid) Stewart Superior Corp.; (Key Lime Pie, Electric Blue shimmer spray) Tattered Angels  *Embossing powder:* (clear) Ranger Industries  *Accent:* (manila tag) Stampers Anonymous  *Sticker:* (butterfly) GCD Studios  *Fibers:* (turquoise ribbon) Michaels; (brown twine) May Arts

## :5: Own Wings Card

**Designer:** Ashley Harris

1. Make card from cardstock.
2. Spritz with shimmer spray; let dry.
3. Stamp bird and sentiment; adhere rhinestones.
4. Border-punch cardstock strip; adhere. Tie on ribbon bow.

*Finished size: 4" x 6"*

## :5: Best Ever Card

**Designer:** Brenda Weaver

1. Make card from cardstock; adhere patterned paper strips.
2. Stamp Circle Doily on specialty paper repeatedly; emboss. Spritz with shimmer sprays and let dry.
3. Trim piece, tie on ribbon bow, and adhere to card.
4. Stamp sentiment.

*Finished size: 5½" x 4¼"*

**SUPPLIES:** *Clear stamps:* (bird, sentiment from Aviary set) Technique Tuesday *Dye ink:* (black) Stewart Superior Corp. *Specialty ink:* (Peacock shimmer spray) Tattered Angels *Cardstock:* (white) Bazzill Basics Paper *Accents:* (aqua rhinestones) Kaisercraft *Fibers:* (aqua ribbon) Offray *Tool:* (border punch) Stampin' Up!

**SUPPLIES:** *Clear stamps:* (Circle Doily) Hero Arts; (sentiment from Big & Bold Wishes set) Papertrey Ink *Dye ink:* (black) Stampin' Up! *Watermark ink:* Tsukineko *Specialty ink:* (Jazz Blue, Patina, Frozen Lake shimmer spray) Tattered Angels *Embossing powder:* (white) Stampin' Up! *Cardstock:* (white) Papertrey Ink *Patterned paper:* (Poll from Basics collection) BasicGrey; (Announce from Avignon collection) 7gypsies *Specialty paper:* (watercolor) Stampin' Up! *Fibers:* (tan stitched ribbon) Papertrey Ink

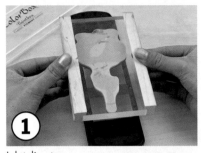

**1** Ink tulip stamp.

**2** To avoid distinct lines, as shown in photo, shift stamp down about ⅛", touch inkpad again.

**3** Stamp tulip on card.

## 5 STEPS Your Own Joy Card

Designer: Maren Benedict

**1** Make card from cardstock.

**2** Create stamped element, following figures 1–3.

**3** Stamp thankful and tie on ribbon bows.

**4** Round bottom corner.

*Finished size: 3¾" x 5½"*

---

DESIGNER TIP

Pre-made spectrum ink pads make gradient stamping quick and easy!

---

**SUPPLIES:** *Rubber stamps:* (tulip from Be Bold set, thankful from When I Am with You set) Unity Stamp Co. *Pigment ink:* (Bright spectrum) Clearsnap *Specialty ink:* (True Black hybrid) Papertrey Ink *Cardstock:* (cream) *Fibers:* (orange ribbon) American Crafts; (yellow twill) Papertrey Ink *Tool:* (corner rounder punch) Creative Memories

**1** Ink dotted apple with light ink and roll edges in dark ink; stamp on cardstock. Repeat. Stamp stems, leaves, and teacher.

**2** Apply teacher mask, stamp apple outline. Remove mask.

**3** Repeat Step 1 with different colored ink.

## Teacher Note Holder

**Designer:** Andrea Vernagus

❶ Create stamped element, following figures 1–3.

❷ Color stem and leaf with silver pen; mat panel with cardstock and insert into acrylic frame.

❸ Mat repositionable notes with cardstock; adhere.

❹ Trim cardstock into tag. Ink dotted apple with light ink and roll edges in dark ink; stamp on cardstock. Stamp stem, leaf, and sentiment. Tie to frame with ribbon.

*Finished size: 5" x 7"*

BONUS IDEA

Create a coordinating pen! Use the same technique to stamp a strip of cardstock. Place your stamped cardstock inside a pen and attach it to the back of your frame with a cardstock loop.

**SUPPLIES:** *Clear stamps:* (dotted apple, stem, leaf, apple outline, teacher, sentiment from Teacher's Apple set) Papertrey Ink *Dye ink:* (Baja Breeze, Not Quite Navy, Certainly Celery, Garden Green, So Saffron, More Mustard, Cameo Coral, Ruby Red, Basic Black) Stampin' Up! *Cardstock:* (Whisper White, Basic Black) Stampin' Up! *Color medium:* (silver pen) Sakura *Fibers:* (black ribbon) Offray *Other:* (repositionable notes, acrylic frame)

① Stamp spiders and spooky on cardstock strip, fully inked.

② Stamp spiders and spooky after off-stamping once.

③ Stamp spiders and spooky after off-stamping twice.

## Spooky Boo Card

**Designer: Latisha Yoast**

❶ Make card from cardstock; adhere patterned paper rectangle.

❷ Create stamped element, following figures 1–3.

❸ Border-punch panel, ink edges, and tie on ribbon bow. Adhere to card with foam tape.

❹ Die-cut and emboss tag from cardstock. Stamp off spiders and spooky on scrap paper (see Designer Tips); stamp on tag. Stamp bats and boo!.

❺ Ink edges of tag and tie onto bow with twine.

*Finished size: 2¾" x 5½"*

**SUPPLIES:** *Clear stamps:* (spider, spooky, bats, boo! from Halloween Party set) Waltzingmouse Stamps *Dye ink:* (Antique Linen, Spiced Marmalade) Ranger Industries; (Basic Black) Stampin' Up! *Cardstock:* (Ivory) Flourishes *Patterned paper:* (Wonderland Classifieds from Hallowe'en in Wonderland collection) Graphic 45 *Fibers:* (cream ribbon) Stampin' Up!; (white jute twine) May Arts *Die:* (tag) Spellbinders *Tool:* (border punch) Fiskars

Apply ink across stamp to create three blocks of color.

Stamp inked image on card.

Stamp sentiment on card.

## :5: Thoughts & Prayers Card

Designer: Teri Anderson

1. Make card from cardstock.
2. Create stamped element, following figures 1–3.
3. Adhere pearls.

*Finished size: 4¼" x 5½"*

**SUPPLIES:** *Rubber stamp:* (Starburst Lace) Hero Arts  *Clear stamp:* (sentiment from Sentimentally Yours set) Technique Tuesday  *Dye ink:* (Sunny Yellow, Bubblegum, Blush) Close To My Heart; (Basic Black) Stampin' Up!  *Cardstock:* (white) Georgia-Pacific  *Accents:* (white pearls) Kaisercraft

HOW TO APPLY INK
Apply ink according to color, from lightest to darkest.

## Celebrate Autumn Card

**Designer:** Julie E. Smith

1. Make card from cardstock.
2. Die-cut leaves and label from cardstock. Stamp leaves, frame, and celebrate autumn on die cuts.
3. Adhere leaves. Tie on twine.
4. Adhere frame with foam tape. Adhere pearls.

*Finished size: 4¼" x 5½"*

## Get Better Soon Card

**Designer:** Jennie Harper

1. Make card from cardstock.
2. Stamp damask repeatedly on cardstock panel; stamp sentiment. Mat with cardstock.
3. Adhere ribbon.
4. Thread button with ribbon; tie. Adhere.
5. Adhere panel with foam tape.

*Finished size: 4¼" x 5½"*

**SUPPLIES:** *Clear stamps:* (leaf solid, lines from Leaf Prints set; frame, celebrate autumn from Fillable Frames #7 set) Papertrey Ink *Dye ink:* (So Saffron, More Mustard, Old Olive, Always Artichoke, Pumpkin Pie, Riding Hood Red, Soft Suede) Stampin' Up! *Cardstock:* (Rustic Cream) Papertrey Ink; (white) Georgia-Pacific *Accents:* (gold pearls) *Fibers:* (jute twine) Papertrey Ink *Dies:* (leaf, label) Papertrey Ink

**SUPPLIES:** *Rubber stamp:* (sentiment from Fanciful Tags set) Gina K Designs *Clear stamp:* (damask from Touch of Elegance set) Layers of Color *Dye ink:* (Spectrum, Autumn Leaves, black) Tsukineko *Cardstock:* (Lipstick Red, Black Onyx, Ivory) Gina K Designs *Accent:* (cream button) Gina K Designs *Fibers:* (black stitched ribbon) Gina K Designs; (black ribbon) May Arts

HOW TO APPLY INK
Apply ink with a sponge to achieve a gradient look.

## 5 Hostess Bag

**Designer: Lisa Johnson**

1. Stamp leaves and sentiment on cardstock panel; ink edges.
2. Die-cut scalloped border from patterned paper; adhere behind panel.
3. Wrap twine around panel. Thread buttons with twine and adhere. Adhere panel to bag with foam tape.

*Finished size: 4¼" x 9½"*

## Happy Birthday Gift Bag

**Designer: Kalyn Kepner**

1. Adhere cardstock and patterned paper panels to bag.
2. Print "Happy birthday" on cardstock; stitch edges. Mat with cardstock; trim with decorative-edge scissors.
3. Punch cardstock strip and adhere behind piece.
4. Stamp feather on cardstock. Trim and adhere with foam tape.
5. Adhere button. Attach brad.
6. Tie on ribbon. Adhere rhinestones. Adhere piece with foam tape.

*Finished size: 4" x 5¼"*

**SUPPLIES:** All supplies from Papertrey Ink unless otherwise noted. *Clear stamps:* (sentiment from Mega Mixed Messages set; leaf solid, lines from Leaf Prints set) *Dye ink:* (Dark Brown, Shades of Gold) Marvy Uchida *Cardstock:* (Rustic Cream) *Patterned paper:* (orange grid from Autumn Abundance pad) *Accents:* (brown buttons) *Fibers:* (natural jute twine) *Die:* (scalloped border) *Other:* (kraft bag) no source

**SUPPLIES:** *Clear stamp:* (feather from Gem Stone Birds set) Inkadinkado *Dye ink:* (Ocean Blue) Inkadinkado; (orange) *Cardstock:* (teal, white) Bazzill Basics Paper; (blue) Wausau Paper *Patterned paper:* (Sage from Green at Heart collection) BasicGrey *Accents:* (orange button) Papertrey Ink; (orange rhinestone, teal decorative brad) K&Company; (teal rhinestone) Queen & Co. *Fibers:* (teal stitched ribbon) Papertrey Ink *Font:* (Chicago House) www.dafont.com *Tools:* (border punch) Martha Stewart Crafts; (decorative-edge scissors) Provo Craft *Other:* (white gift bag)

### ⟨5⟩ Little Birdie Card
**Designer:** Cristina Kowalczyk

❶ Make card from cardstock.

❷ Adhere patterned paper rectangle.

❸ Tie on ribbon.

❹ Stamp birds and sentiment on cardstock. Adhere with foam tape.

*Finished size: 5½" x 4¼"*

### ⟨5⟩ Hello Hello Card
**Designer:** Sarah Jay

❶ Make card from cardstock; punch bottom edge of front flap.

❷ Stamp hello. repeatedly on card.

❸ Adhere cardstock behind punched edge.

*Finished size: 3½" x 5"*

**SUPPLIES:** *Clear stamps:* (bird, sentiment from Sentiments Large set) American Crafts *Dye ink:* (Rose Bud, Lilac Posies, Grape Jelly) Tsukineko *Cardstock:* (white) Papertrey Ink *Patterned paper:* (Buttercup Dot from Double Dot collection) BoBunny Press *Fibers:* (teal ribbon) Stampin' Up!

**SUPPLIES:** *Rubber stamp:* (hello.) Studio G *Dye ink:* (Angel Pink, Rose Bud, Lady Bug, Tangelo, Cantaloupe) Tsukineko *Cardstock:* (Raspberry) Memory Box; (white) Stampin' Up! *Tool:* (border punch) EK Success

DESIGNER TIP
Be sure to remove excess ink from
rectangle with a moist cotton swab.

## Miss You Card
**Designer:** AJ Otto

1. Make card from cardstock; spray with ink.
2. Tie on twill.
3. Die-cut and dry-emboss circle, rectangle, and scalloped rectangle from cardstock.
4. Stamp branch on rectangle; heat-emboss. Spray with ink. Mat with scalloped rectangle and adhere with foam tape.
5. Stamp miss you on cardstock circle; adhere with foam tape. Adhere rhinestones.

*Finished size: 4¼" x 5½"*

## Mon Amie Card
**Designer:** Belinda Chang Langner

1. Make card from cardstock. Round bottom corners.
2. Stamp lace border repeatedly on card.
3. Stamp sentiment on card.
4. Tie on ribbon.

*Finished size: 4½" x 5½"*

**SUPPLIES:** *Rubber stamps:* (miss you, branch from Botanicals set) Gina K Designs *Pigment ink:* (Fresh Snow, Raspberry Fizz) Papertrey Ink *Specialty ink:* (Black Cherry, Meadow Green, Lemongrass, Coral Reef shimmer spray) Tattered Angels *Embossing powder:* (clear) Jo-Ann Stores *Cardstock:* (white) Neenah Paper *Accents:* (pink rhinestones) Kaisercraft *Fibers:* (white twill) Papertrey Ink *Dies:* (circle, rectangle, scalloped rectangle) Spellbinders

**SUPPLIES:** *Clear stamps:* (lace border from Victorian Frippery set; mon amie from Fancy Phrases set) Waltzingmouse Stamps *Pigment ink:* (Sweet Blush, Hibiscus Burst, Raspberry Fizz) Papertrey Ink *Specialty ink:* (Pure Poppy hybrid) Papertrey Ink *Cardstock:* (white) Papertrey Ink *Fibers:* (pink ribbon) Papertrey Ink *Tool:* (corner rounder punch) We R Memory Keepers

# Index

# Patterns

## THANK YOU TEACHER CARD
p.34
Designer: Kim Hughes

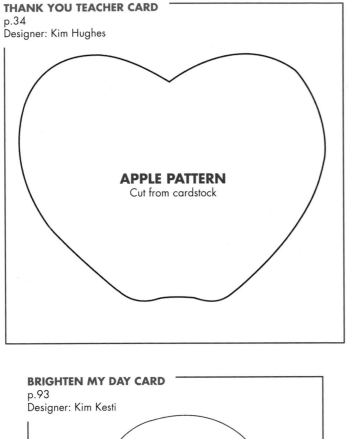

**APPLE PATTERN**
Cut from cardstock

## THANKS A TON CARD
p.102
Designer: Beth Opel

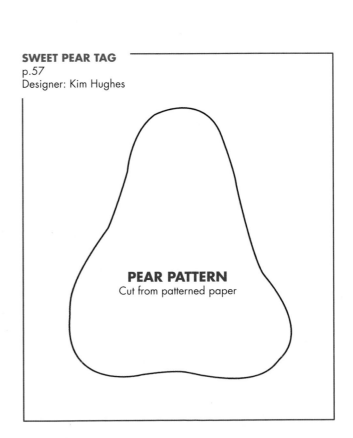

**WEIGHT**
Cut from kraft cardstock

**WEIGHT SHADOW**
Cut from brown cardstock

## BRIGHTEN MY DAY CARD
p.93
Designer: Kim Kesti

**BULB**
Cut from white cardstock

**SCREW CAP**
Cut from silver metallic cardstock

## SWEET PEAR TAG
p.57
Designer: Kim Hughes

**PEAR PATTERN**
Cut from patterned paper